A Guide to Parenting in Islam

Cherishing Childhood

Dr. Muhammad Abdul Bari

Ta-Ha Publishers Ltd.

First Published as
'The Greatest Gift: A Guide to Parenting from an Islamic Perspective'
in Rabi al-Awwal 1419AH/July 1998 CE

Revised and published as this edition in 1436AH/January 2015

Ta-Ha Publishers Ltd.
Unit 4, The Windsor Centre,
Windsor Grove,
London, SE27 9NT
United Kingdom

Website: **www.tahapublishers.com**
Email: support@tahapublishers.com

Written by: **Dr. Muhammad Abdul Bari**
General Editor: **Dr. Abia Afsar-Siddiqui**
Book/Cover Design and Typeset by: **Shakir Abdulcadir .: opensquares.uk**

A catalogue record of this book is available from the British Library

ISBN: 978-1-84200-154-7

Printed and Bound by: IMAK Ofset, Turkey

Contents

Acknowledgements

This book is the outcome of my long-term involvement in youth and community work in Britain. Many people, including the very young and old, have contributed to the ideas contained in it. They all deserve my sincere thanks. The decision to write a book on parenting was further enhanced when I came across a respected elder who had 'lost' his daughter. I was not sure how to comfort him at that time. I pray to Allah that no one falls in that situation with their children. The pressure within me to start writing became stronger when I was approached by the Witness Pioneer network, an internet based virtual organisation, to run a course on some social issues for their virtual school. I made up my mind to run the 'Islamic Perspective of Parenting' course. I am indebted to them for giving me that opportunity, through which I learnt a lot. I am also grateful to Dr. Jamil Sherif of Webstar

Plc, London, who decided to run the same course on their Salaam web page with additional online question and answer facilities. In the same way, my participation in a week-long Facilitator Course on 'Strengthening Families and Strengthening Communities: An Inclusive Parent Programme' by the Race Equality Unit (REU) in London was useful.

I express my deep appreciation for the contribution of my wife Sayeda, for her understanding, support and contributions to the writing of the book. In spite of the pressure of life, her excellent family management and sense of humour continuously encouraged me to sit at the computer. I am grateful to our four children, Rima, Raiyan, Labib and Adib for their enthusiasm during the process of writing. I am also indebted to a number of *'ulema* for helping me to find references from the Qur'an and books of hadith. May Allah shower His blessings upon all of them.

Preface

"If you are planning for a year, plant grain. If you are planning for a decade, plant trees. But if you are planning for a millennium, then plant human beings."

In every culture, the birth of a new born baby brings great joy. The arrival of a helpless little being signals an irreversible life change for its parents and wider family, as well as fresh hope for the future. This is a blank canvas that has the potential to blossom or wilt depending on the environment that it is nurtured in – like a plant in a pot.

It is all too easy in the early years of a child's life to be engrossed in the physical care of a baby. After all, this small human being is utterly dependent and it is exhausting for the parents to simply keep up with the seemingly constant cycle of feeding, dressing, bathing and sleeping their precious one. But parenting is much more than that.

Children have the fundamental right to receive physical, intellectual, emotional AND spiritual nourishment from their parents, and it is this, that makes parenting such a dynamic and challenging enterprise. Positive parenting is fundamental to raising children in any society. It is proactive and responsive, rather than reactive and rigid. Islam's approach to life is holistic and that includes the parental responsibility entrusted by Allah. With its transcendental value-system and its crystal-clear focus on life, Islam has a unique way of preparing the younger generation for their future roles. The hadith that 'no parent can give their child a better gift than good manners, good character and a good education'[1] puts a heavy burden on Muslim parents to invest in their children. To be a parent is to be a father or mother, educator, mentor, guide and role model to children; to build a long-lasting parent-child relationship based on mutual love, respect and loyalty.

It is a grave mistake to believe that it is too early in a child's life to put positive and proactive parenting into practice or that a child is too young to receive spiritual nourishment. The longest of journeys begins with the first step and the first steps to parenting should ideally begin even before a child is born. Our children are the greatest asset we will ever be entrusted with. Invest time, effort and thought into them wisely and the rewards are bountiful in this life and in the Hereafter. If we give greater importance to our material assets – our homes, possessions and careers – then we will be the biggest losers, for we will have 'lost' our children in the sea of *jahiliyyah* (ignorance) that surrounds us.

Many Muslim parents are either unaware of the depth of the challenges or are too simplistic in dealing with their young ones. *A Guide to Parenting in Islam: Cherishing Childhood* is my humble contribution to those Muslim parents who realise that parenting is a mission to recreate a new generation of human beings in the model of

1. At-Tirmidhi

the righteous predecessors of Islam; a weighty responsibility for which we will be held accountable on the Day of Judgement.

The nature of the book is reader-friendly and not academic or scholarly. The principle followed is holistic and preventative, rather than piecemeal and curative. Human life is complex and as such there are many approaches to addressing an issue, depending on cultural or other variations. I have followed the broad Islamic principle that anything not forbidden in Islam is acceptable. The book is about facing or addressing the challenges of parenting from an Islamic perspective. It is not meant to be a book of *fiqh*.

This book is primarily written for Muslims who are in minority situations, mainly in the West.[2] This should not, I think, jeopardise the common appeal of the book and I hope that any reader can benefit from it. The attempt to criticise the post-modern West has been done in context and as objectively as possible. In the same manner, the Muslim world and the East have also been criticised. The purpose is to put forward the best of both. I apologise if I have failed in that objectivity.

I have addressed the realities, issues and challenges of adolescence in contemporary social life in my companion book, *A Guide to Parenting in Islam: Addressing Adolescence*. Both books are complementary in many ways and parents are advised to go through both of them together in order to gain a wider and long-term perspective on parenting.

My passion in writing this book is to create more awareness in as many Muslim parents as possible and take them through the complex but essential journey of parenting in this unpredictable social milieu.

2. It is accepted that the word 'West' is not limited to geographical boundary. In referring to the West, the European, North American and Australasian countries are included. However, due to globalisation in recent decades the discussion on East or West has essentially become pedantic as more Muslims permanently live in Europe, America and Australia than in some Muslim countries. Similarly, many indigenous Westerners also now live in the East and/or Muslim countries.

It is an attempt to regenerate the Muslim communities of the West through 'common-sense' parenting. This is a 'parent to parent book' not an expert to layperson' one. My credential is my continuous work in the grass-roots Muslim communities and my fervent desire to be a better parent by facilitating numerous parenting courses over the years. I rely on the forgiveness of Allah for my shortcomings and pray that He accepts this humble work.

Chapter One

A Trust From Allah

You, who believe! Do not betray Allah and His Messenger, and do not knowingly betray your trusts. (Qur'an 8:27)

CHILDREN AS A 'TRUST' AND A 'TEST'

A child is a Trust from Allah ('Amanah' in Arabic). In other words, a child is entrusted into the care of parents by Allah and those parents are responsible in the eyes of Allah to take care of that trust to the best of their ability. Quite simply, to fail to look after that trust is to betray the trust of Allah in one of the worst possible ways. It is therefore essential if we wish to raise our standing in the eyes of Allah, to complete this task to the best of our ability and the first step in this direction is an understanding of the nature of the task of parenting - the rewards and the trials.

Knowledgeable Muslim men and women know what is important in life in order to attain success in this world and the Hereafter. Thus, they realise that it is not enough to simply feed, clothe and provide material things for a child. They also nourish them with moral and spiritual teachings and examples so that they may grow up to be good human beings for society and obedient and willing slaves of Allah. Their 'parenting' encompasses all that is good for their children in this world and in the Hereafter, which in turn is also good for the parents in this world and the Hereafter. In this mundane world they are blessed with peace, tranquillity and pleasure in life and in the eternal world they will see the fruits of their parenting efforts.

> ***A slave will have his rank raised and will say: 'O my Lord how has this come about for me?' He will say: 'Through your sons after you, seeking forgiveness for you.'*** (Ahmad and Ibn Majah)

While the rewards of parenting are great, so too can be the trials along the way. There are the physical demands, particularly on the mother, of looking after a dependent, helpless baby. As children grow, their parents ride the emotional rollercoaster of ill health, academic worries and social concerns that might present themselves throughout a child's life. Throughout these periods, steadfast Muslims know that the reason that they have been created is to worship Allah and they do not allow their children or other worldly matters to divert themselves from this central task.

> **You who believe! Do not let your wealth or children divert you from the remembrance of Allah. Whoever does that is lost.** (Qur'an 63:9)

This means that the believer is grateful to Allah for any pleasure that he receives from his child and is patient when his child is a source of worry or grief.

A MONUMENTAL TASK

Parenting is not merely parenthood. The latter is primarily a biological process, while the former is a conscious act of embarking on a life process - a process whereby an adult human being is responsible for the physical, emotional, spiritual and intellectual nourishment and development of another small individual. Parenting is a task that demands emotional, psychological and spiritual maturity as the parent must also be a teacher, mentor and spiritual guide.

Of course, parents are human beings with limitations and, as such, cannot be 'perfect' in rearing their children. No parent will be chastised on the Day of Judgement for unintentional mistakes in raising their children, as human beings are born with natural frailties. Parents do, however, need to be better aware that on their weak shoulders rest the burdens of raising 'human beings', Allah's emissaries on earth.

The family is the microcosm of the community, a wider world, where duties and responsibilities are exercised in accordance with the commands of Allah. Love, passion, compromise, sacrifice and other human features tie the members of the family together with a common sense of purpose. In any civilisation, it is the family, not the individual, that is the unit upon which society rests. With the arrival of a new baby, a new family unit is created. The role of parents is to ensure that the new family functions to the benefit of all its constituent members and to provide an environment that nourishes all the needs of the children at each stage in their lives, so that they are, in turn, well equipped to form the basis of a healthy new family of the next generation.

This is easier said than done and the parenting journey is full of ups and downs, surprises and challenges that shape the personality of the parents as well as the children. Honest and self-aware parents will make a determined effort to plan and give thought to their role as parents rather than just ambling through life without a serious appreciation of the depth of the responsibility they have been blessed with. This is akin to setting out on a journey through unknown territory without a map or a compass!

The mother and father form a team with complementary skills and natures, both of which are needed to bring up a child. While some jobs are better suited to the mother, the overall job of parenting is a shared one. Thus it is important that both parents have a shared vision of the destination they wish to reach and how they plan to get there. A lack of team planning can lead to disharmony and confusion for the whole family unit. 'If you fail to prepare; prepare to fail'; we are often good at applying this adage to our work lives or other life projects. We expect our children's teachers to spend a considerable amount of time preparing and planning their lessons but we manage to ignore it when it comes to bringing up our own children. Therefore in order to get the best out of the parenting experience as well as fulfilling their child's potential, wise parents will give thought to the task ahead of them.

That is not to say that those parents will not make mistakes – we all will – but the thoughtful parent is more likely to acknowledge their shortcomings, learn through the process and adapt in such a way as to cause the least harm to their offspring and to the stability of the family unit. The Prophet Muhammad ﷺ has mentioned:

> ***Every one of you is a shepherd and everyone is responsible for what he is shepherd of.*** (al-Bukhari and Muslim)

KEEP AWAY FROM THE FIRE

> **O you who believe! Safeguard yourselves and your families from a Fire whose fuel is people and stones.** (Qur'an 66:6)

This verse contains the essence and meaning of the divine responsibility laid upon Muslims. It is a moral and social obligation for a Muslim to enjoin good and forbid wrongdoing to those with whom they have close links. As custodians of our children, this has direct implications and a special significance for them. Parental duty is at the heart of Muslim life. For a sound and healthy continuity of the true essence of Islam, every parent must transfer the spirit and message of Islam to their offspring.

If an individual parent cannot cope with this onerous and demanding task for some reason, then the wider community has to create networks so that nobody falls through the net. Like any other community, there will be 'weaker' Muslims, but the wider community must establish the necessary infrastructure to lend them support. While parenting children is a task for the parents of that child, it is nevertheless the collective responsibility of society to ensure that individuals are supported in such a way that they can carry out their duties to the best of their abilities. Although according to the Qur'an, nobody bears the burden of others nor are they burdened with unbearable burdens, human beings have a greater responsibility involving their families and communities, society and humanity at large.[1]

HUMAN BEINGS AS SOCIAL BEINGS

The mother and father are filled with passionate anticipation and excitement at the arrival of a baby. They are ready to provide the new addition with support and nourishment, not out of duty but out of impulsive emotion and unfathomable love. The relationship between

1. Family, in the Islamic context, is far wider than the so-called modern 'nuclear family' or even the extended family. The Qur'anic term '*ahl*' or 'family' can mean 'people of the same faith' or 'comrades'. In practical day-to-day life it means people close to oneself - relatives through blood or marriage, neighbours, dependants, friends, colleagues, etc. It includes people who share one's race, tribe, culture and faith. As a result, the Muslim responsibility for their 'family' is immense and one that encompasses their life-mission.

parents and children is at the heart of a family. When this love is pure and strong, it filters out to encompass love for brothers, sisters, uncles, aunts and so on.

The old saying, 'human beings are social beings' represents the idea that healthy human beings have relationships in which they fulfil their duties to others as well as deriving pleasure from these social interactions. Indeed, fulfilling the rights of others, helping people and serving the community with no expectation of thanks is a part of the *deen*. It fulfils the twin purposes of both securing the pleasure of Allah and bringing peace to society.

In an individualistic society, human beings live selfishly to gratify their own desires. While each person may think they are 'happy', the net result is a departure from basic humanity and a society that is avaricious and perilously competitive. They are features of materialism in which human beings vie with each other to compete and triumph. This gives rise to the 'survival of the fittest' attitude that makes some people super rich and powerful at the expense of the vast majority. Such a society can never prosper because the super-rich have lost their morals in their struggle to gain material wealth while the rest of society is selling its soul to reach that 'elite' status. Countless social problems seep in and cripple such a society to the point that society is chaotic and, ironically, individuals are not happy either.

In contrast, Islam advocates social responsibility without, of course, endangering individual creativity and innovation. It teaches patience and gratitude rather than instant self-gratification. Similarly, in order for our parenting to be the best that it can be, we must not only look at our child as an individual to be parented by two other individuals, but to view the family unit as a building block within society. When every family within a society views itself as part of a cohesive mass, working together for the collective good, then society will have elevated itself to the very best it can be.

POSITIVE PARENTING: A CREATIVE ENDEAVOUR

Plants in the nursery and children in the home and school 'nursery' have striking similarities. The culmination of a plant is a healthy tree with flowers and fruit. Similarly, the culmination of a child is a successful and balanced human being. Just as a neglected or partially neglected plant will grow with deficiencies, so a neglected child can reach adulthood with psychological issues and a self-destructive lifestyle. Parental care does not simply mean providing children with good food, clothing and a roof over their heads. Care extends to empathy, understanding, emotional support, instilling moral values and giving children the tools to negotiate their way in the world. Parental care is about providing a warm, safe and harmonious environment within the home that fills the child with confidence and love that they can then pass on to others. If each family unit can sow the seed of virtue, then collectively society will reap the fruits. This ideal can only be achieved with planning, hard work and a partnership, not only within each family unit but also between families, in other words, by implementing positive parenting.

Unfortunately, most parents fall into the trap of 'accidental' parenting. They have no idea of the enormity of the privilege and responsibility they have been granted by Allah. They fulfil the basic material needs of their children but starve them spiritually until their child hits a social or psychological problem. At this point, the 'accidental' parent reacts heavy-handedly and impulsively, often alienating their offspring. In a competitive society, parents try to hide their shortcomings from the wider community for fear of shame.

Positive parenting is essentially the opposite of this. Positive parents engage with their children from the earliest age. They are on hand to nip any potential problems in the bud and when they find that they need support, they can rely on like-minded, empathetic families for backing. Like any creative endeavour it is a challenging task but it is made easier when parents view their children as their partners – people that they can work with rather than constantly arguing with or telling off. Positive parenting takes the proactive rather than reactive approach, preventing issues reaching a head, and being flexible and gentle in dealing with children rather than harsh and rigid to encourage inclusion rather than alienation. It is no coincidence that often the most alienated and disaffected members of society display anti-social or criminal behaviour. A parent can only do their best – the rest lies in Allah's hands.

CAUSES OF POOR PARENTING

Along the parenting journey, there are some common stumbling blocks that parents must beware of falling into:

■ Ignorance

It is dangerous in the extreme to assume that once children arrive in this world, things will somehow fall into place and children will follow in their parents' footsteps. Parenting is an endeavour that requires thought, planning and hard work just like any other major life project. To ignore this fact is to endanger the future of our children.

This does not mean that parents need a string of formal degrees and qualifications to raise their children. It does means, though, that parents must arm themselves with:

- an understanding of the purpose of creation, so that they can guide their children as to how best to serve Allah;
- knowledge of the society they live in and current issues, so they can raise a child that is self-fulfilled as well as being a productive member of the family, community and society at large.

■ Complacency

When parents hear of teenagers who have fallen into bad company, become addicts, or carry out anti-social behaviour, it is easy to think, 'That won't happen to my child'. The reality is that dangers lurk everywhere in society, and with the advent of the internet, those dangers are inside our homes as well. It is important for parents to make their children aware of the potential pitfalls at an appropriate age and then to keep a constant, yet trusting eye over their children.

■ Indifference

A parent should not only be aware of the emotional, intellectual, physical and spiritual needs of a growing child, but also begin to fulfil all of these from the first day. Indifferent parents may be aware of their child's needs but they procrastinate and believe that they can deal with certain issues when the child is older. But this too late. When a child is older, their character is already formed but parents have missed the opportunity to make a positive contribution to their child's personality.

■ Lack of Experience

Of course, new parents lack experience, but parenting is a steep learning curve. We live in a society where information is abundant and opportunities are available for those who wish to avail them. Parents can learn from their own experience of being parented and the more experienced parents in their community. Lack of experience should not be a valid excuse.

■ Inherited Methods of Parenting

While the spirit of parenting and vision of Muslim life always remains the same, techniques and approaches have to be adapted to mould with the changing society that we live in. Many Muslim parents of today have a background in which their own parents or grandparents were brought up in a different country or with a different set of circumstances. This may not necessarily be appropriate for the next generation.

■ Family Misfortune

Accidents, mishaps and misfortune can strike a family without warning, leaving a legacy of distress or long-term hardship. In any event, a domestic problem puts extreme pressure on the single parent, who may find it difficult to juggle all their responsibilities without the support of a spouse. As far as possible, wider family and societal support is needed so that children are cushioned from their loss and the weighty responsibility of parenting is not left solely on the shoulders of one parent.

■ Pressures of Life

Modern life is a rat race. Parents are overwhelmed with financial and career responsibilities and social commitments. It can be difficult to keep the various roles balanced and, sadly, it is too easy to let a young child's spiritual well-being slip down the list of priorities in life. It is a fact that people make time for the things they consider important. A child is the greatest asset and investment that a parent will ever have. It reaps greater rewards than wealth and property and career status. To prioritise any of these over a child would surely be the greatest folly.

PREPARING THEM FOR GREAT THINGS

Muslim parents raising children as a minority in a challenging environment have a doubly formidable task before them. Islam's main goal is to create a world where human beings are liberated from the clutches of ignorance, *jahiliyyah*, and the first step in achieving this is to educate and liberate the mind before all else. Contrary to the common perception of today, one's practice of Islam demands intellectual exercise in every area of knowledge, from aesthetics to zoology. Islam's assertive approach to life encourages Muslims to take an active role in intellectual and social enterprises; to participate in, interact and engage with wider society at every level for the common good. The key is to be an active and valued contributor to society rather than a passive bystander.

Muslims in the past played a pivotal role on the world stage, even where they were a tiny minority and insignificant in number. They were pioneers in passing on the true essence of Islam to their own children on the one hand, and to the rest of humanity on the other. Together they expanded the frontiers of a civilisation dedicated to the divine, without coercion. Multitudes of men, women and children came to Islam because of the character and nobility of existing Muslims. Islam gave peace to the hearts of these people and harmony to diverse and multi-faith societies.

Parents need to prepare their children with this broadest aim in mind; to be passionate about making a positive difference. For our children to stand tall, we should give them the foundation of a stable and loving family environment to stand upon, and educate their minds and hearts with knowledge of the *deen* and the *dunya*. We should encourage them to set worthy and lofty goals in their lives; goals that leave a legacy rather than simply satisfying worldly desires of status and wealth.

As daunting as this may seem, every journey consists of small and manageable steps at every stage and in the remainder of this book, I hope to lay the crumbs that provide food for thought for the positive parent.

Chapter Two

Parenthood and the Age of Nurturing

Narrated Abu Huraira ﷺ: ***I heard Allah's Apostle ﷺ saying, "Allah divided mercy into one hundred parts and He kept its ninety-nine parts with him and sent down its one part on the earth, and because of that one single part, His Creations are merciful to each other, so that even the mare lifts up its hoof away from its baby, lest she should trample on it."*** (al-Bukhari)

MARRIAGE, FAMILY AND PARENTHOOD

The first step in parenthood is, in fact, marriage. Marriage provides solace, comfort and pleasure to two adults. It also teaches compromise and sacrifice in order to live together under one roof. The sort of spouses people wish to marry reveals what sort of children they want to have. Truthful, honest and believing men and women will look for those very same qualities in their partners. On the other hand, indecent partners will naturally cling to one another (Qur'an 24:26).

Marriage is a lifelong commitment between two people and the union of two families. It is the foundation upon which future generations will anchor themselves and so it must be strong. The strength of a marriage derives from:

- love and mercy
- respect and affection
- steadfastness and forgiveness
- justice and fairness
- honesty and integrity
- openness and clarity
- mutual consultation
- loyalty
- sacrifice
- hard work and dedication.

When these qualities are present and the bond between husband and wife is strong, this is the ideal environment in which to nurture a baby.

Stepping onto the road to parenthood is a unique and adventurous journey; fascinating for the newly married couple with their first baby. The parents-to-be can join pre-natal groups and read books on the subject, all of which are very valuable, but at the end of the day, it is a role that experience teaches best. The most important resources needed for this job are reliance in Allah (*tawakkul*), reliance on your own natural instinct to help you cope and succeed, plenty of common sense, an open and exploratory mind and lots of patience.

Tawakkul solves many problems. It is never the 'perfect' time to have a baby in terms of career, finances and so on. Of course, a husband and wife should work hard to create the best possible environment that minimises the challenges of parenthood, both before and after the birth. However, the rest lies with Allah. *Tawakkul* should be accompanied by maximum effort and constant supplication to Him.

Then when you have reached a firm decision, put your trust in Allah. Allah loves those who put their trust in him. (Qur'an 3:159)

PLANNING FOR THE FAMILY

Pregnancy is undoubtedly a very unique time for both parents. It is an exciting time as well as an anxious one for the parents who hope and pray for the safe arrival of a normal and healthy baby. It is also the perfect time for parents to plan and prepare for the arrival of their little one. This may involve reading up about the developing stages of the foetus, the birthing process, researching the various accessories that will be needed once the baby arrives and so on.

However involved the father is during pregnancy, this is one life experience that can only be experienced by a woman. It is the woman who goes through the hardships and pain of carrying a baby and giving birth. This is why the mother's position in Islam in higher than the father's. For fathers, parenthood begins at the point that the child is born and they can physically connect with their baby. But for a mother, she becomes a parent from the moment she finds out she is pregnant and her sacrifice begins during pregnancy itself. From that moment on, she makes a conscious effort to take care of her health, diet and lifestyle, knowing that whatever she eats and does will impact on the life growing inside her.

Positive parents will also use this time to reflect on the character and values that they would like to see in their children, how they plan to impart these and the various styles of parenting. This is also the time to assess the suitability of the environment that the baby will be welcomed into, not just from a physical point of view but also a spiritual and emotional one. A baby born to loving parents who consciously fear Allah and perform good deeds has, arguably, a better start in life than one who does not. Parents can turn their attention to virtuous and positive thinking, establishing *salah*, offering *sadaqah*, reading the Qur'an and continuous *dhikr* and supplication to Allah. This will not only create the ideal environment for the new arrival to thrive in, but also be of immense benefit to the unborn child. Whatever a mother says, does and thinks impacts on the foetus and provides spiritual nourishment. The key to all of this preparation is the harmony, communication and loving partnership between husband and wife in the service of Allah.

THE NEW ARRIVAL

When a child was born in a family, A'ishah, may Allah be pleased with her, would not ask whether it was a boy or girl, but rather she would ask, 'Is it complete and sound?' So, if she was told that it was, she would say, 'All praise and thanks belong to Allah, Lord of the worlds'. (al-Bukhari)

Meeting your new born for the first time is an indescribable experience and one that no-one ever forgets. Despite what marketing departments may try to tell you, the most important things that the little one needs are a mother's arms, a mother's love and a mother's breast. Skin-to-skin contact and holding the baby close is the most powerful way to reassure them of your presence and love and to provide them with the security they need at their most vulnerable time in a world which is totally new and daunting to them.

The birth of every baby is a miracle of Allah; a tiny helpless being that begins its journey through life as a clean slate, ready to absorb whatever you expose it to. It is an experience that reminds us of our own vulnerability on earth and the temporary nature of existence. We also started life in this way, but with the grace of Allah and the efforts of our parents, we are able to continue the cycle of life. These are moments that should humble us into gratitude to Allah and to our parents and strengthen our resolve to carry out our parental duties in the best possible way.

ISLAMIC CUSTOMS AT THE BIRTH OF A CHILD

The arrival of a child is a glad tiding that needs to be conveyed and shared with others (Qur'an 3:39, 37:101). Indeed the extended family and community will want to share in the new parents' joy and welcome the new arrival with open arms. There may be cultural customs, for example, the distribution of sweets and there is no harm in carrying these out, but the following tasks must be carried out as a matter of priority at the appropriate time.

- ➔ ***Adhan*** – some Islamic schools of thought recommend that a male adult, father or someone close in the family, should recite the *adhan* (call for collective prayer) in the right ear. It is mentioned in a hadith that Shaytan runs away at the sound of the *adhan*. In the world of spirits, human beings declared their instinctive readiness to accept Allah as their Lord (Qur'an 7:172). The first sound to reach the babies' ears should thus be the declaration of Allah's greatness, so that the sound always reverberates in their sub-conscious mind.

  The mother of the faithful, A'ishah, may Allah be pleased with her, mentioned, 'I saw the Prophet ﷺ call the adhan in the ear of al-Hussein ibn 'Ali when his mother, Fatimah, gave birth to him'. (Ahmad, Abu Dawud and at-Tirmidhi)

- ➔ ***Tahneek*** – It is considered by some an excellent practice to give a small amount of chewed date to new born babies, so that their life starts with the taste of sweetness. As life is complex and challenging with adversities and hardships, this gift of sweetness may be useful for their lives.

A'ishah, may Allah be pleased with her, said 'New born children used to be brought to the Messenger of Allah ﷺ and he would supplicate for blessings for them and rub a chewed date upon their palates.' (Muslim and Abu Dawud)

➔ **Removal of Head Hair** – The Prophet ﷺ used to shave the baby's head completely, preferably on the seventh day after birth. It is also advised that the weight of the hairs be balanced with silver and the equivalent to the weight be given in *sadaqah* to the poor.

When al-Hasan ؓ was born, he (the Messenger ﷺ) said to her (Fatimah): ***'Shave his head and give the weight of his hair in silver to the poor.' So, she shaved off his hair, weighed it and its weight was a Dirham or a part of a Dirham.*** (Ahmad and al-Bayhaqi)

➔ ***'Aqiqah*** – It is a Prophetic tradition to perform the *'aqiqah* for a baby and some say that it is on the seventh day after birth. Some regard the Islamic practice as sacrificing two sheep for a boy and one for a girl. As the birth of a child is a happy occasion, friends and families are invited to celebrate the occasion.

Every child is held in pledge for its* 'aqiqah*, which is sacrificed for him on his seventh day and he is named on it and his head is shaved. (Ahmad and Abu Dawud)

Whoever has a child born to him and wishes to offer a sacrifice then let him sacrifice two sheep for a boy and a single sheep for a girl. (Abu Dawud and an-Nasa'i)

With the child there is **'aqiqah** ***[a word for the hair on the head of the new born child and possibly also for the foreskin], so spill blood for him and remove the harm from him.*** (al-Bukhari, Ahmad, Abu Dawud and at-Tirmidhi)

Unfortunately, this Sunnah is not given enough importance in the Muslim communities of the West, perhaps because ordering the sacrifice and distributing the meat is considered too time-consuming. Many people find that an easier solution is to send money to their relatives in other countries who offer sacrifices on their behalf and distribute the meat. As a result, a great occasion for communal celebration is missed and one of the most important rites is outsourced.

➔ **Circumcision** – Circumcision is an accepted practice deriving from Ibrahim عليه السلام. Some people regard it as correct to circumcise the child on the seventh day, others recommend deferring it for some years and preferably until the child loses his first teeth. The following hadith reveals the importance which Islam places on the cleanliness of the human body. Obviously, cleanliness of the soul is equally important.

The **fitrah** ***(the natural way) is five: circumcision, shaving the private parts, trimming the moustache, clipping the nails and plucking hair from the armpits.*** (al-Bukhari and Muslim)

➔ **Naming** – A child has the right to a good name as this is something they will be called by for the rest of their lives. Muslim parents always try to give their children good names with pleasant meanings. Names should be linked with the father's name and be meaningful. Praiseworthy names are those that mean slaves of Allah or of His attributes. They could also follow the names of the Prophets and the notable Muslims of the past. Names with negative connotations or those that have no meaning should be avoided. The Prophet Muhammad ﷺ used to change any name that had unpleasant meanings.

Call them after their fathers. That is closer to justice in the sight of Allah. And if you do not know who their fathers were then they are your brothers in religion and people under your patronage... (Qur'an 33:5)

SIBLING EQUALITY

New arrivals in the house naturally get full attention from all the family, leaving elder siblings feeling a little left out. The previously youngest ones, who had probably so far monopolised parental attention, can be confused or even jealous. Parents have to be sensitive about this and assure them, according to their age and understanding, that the share of their love has not been reduced. In the beginning, new born babies should not be left alone with their immediate elder siblings; parents need to watch out that the older ones do not harm them in any way. It may be helpful to involve elder siblings as 'Mummy's little helper' and give them small age-appropriate responsibilities so they feel needed and develop caring feelings towards the new baby. Over time, sibling love will deepen and parents can encourage siblings to look out for each other.

It goes without saying that it is grossly un-Islamic to discriminate negatively between a boy and a girl. Sons and daughters must be welcomed and treated equally and afforded the same opportunities and parental attention. In the beginning of children's lives there is simply childhood and the issue of boyhood and girlhood becomes distinct later on. The features and demands diverge as the children gradually and naturally acquire and radiate their masculine and feminine qualities. Obviously, during their formative years as females and males, mothers and fathers should respectively address specific gender issues. Conscious parents should carefully watch out for the developmental phases of their children and make sure that equity is maintained. Boys and girls are not the same, but no one is superior to another except in *taqwa*. On the Day of Judgement, human beings are accountable to Allah on the basis of their actions, not gender. The teaching of the Prophet Muhammad ﷺ on this is clear in many traditions. As he did not have any surviving son, his behaviour with his daughter Fatimah, and his other daughters, may Allah be pleased with them, was exemplary.

> ***Treat your children equally.***
> (Ahmad, Abu Dawud and an-Nasa'i)

> ***Whoever takes care of two girls until they reach adulthood he and I will stay on the Day of Rising – and he interlaced his fingers.*** (Muslim)

LOOKING AFTER THE NEW BORN BABY

Looking after a new born baby is an intense experience. Holding your own baby in your arms is exhilarating and one of the most emotionally fulfilling experiences of life. It encompasses all the senses from those special moments of skin-to-skin contact, to that unique smell of a new born, to the quick shallow breaths they take while they sleep. Watching a baby grow and develop is a living miracle. They provide pleasure to the eyes, vigour to the heart and joy to the soul.

On the other hand, their demands are many and unrelenting. No sooner does the mother complete one cycle of feeding, changing and settling the baby than the routine begins again. Coupled with a mother's hormonal changes and the lack of sleep, it is little wonder that mothers feel anything from exhaustion to post-natal depression. It can be all too easy to get trapped into taking care of a baby's day-to-day physical requirements at the expense of other things. At this stage, it is vital that the mother receives the help, support and understanding she needs from her husband and other considerate members of the family.

A mother needs relief from her constant maternal duties in order to carry out her religious duties and in order to rest so that she can be recharged, mentally, emotionally, physically and spiritually. This will give her the strength to be the best, most positive parent she can be. As we mentioned earlier, parenting is much more than ensuring that the physical needs of a child are fulfilled; the new born needs emotional and spiritual nourishment even at this young age and they cannot get this from parents that are themselves drained and exhausted.

While there is no taking away from the fact that it is a relentless task to look after a new born, it may help to consider the situation from a different perspective. Babies have a unique way of communicating their needs to their carers. They recognise their mother, father and other members of the family and gradually learn to behave accordingly. They see, observe, respond and learn. Their hands and feet also participate in their action. They respond to internal signals such as hunger, tiredness, pain and emotional need by crying or changing the intensity of their movement. Externally, they are surrounded by countless images, information and experiences that pile up in their brains and create the beginnings of a unique character. These stimuli will create different responses in every baby, with some being more overwhelmed than others. Babies do not cry without reason and they are not demanding just for the sake of being so; they are simply communicating a need in their own way.

The nurturing parent must be aware that their baby is communicating with them, try to interpret what they are 'saying' and respond to it accordingly. After all, the way parents look after their babies has profound impact on the character of that child and in turn impacts how they will form relationships in the future. A parent who attends to their child is saying, 'I am here for you. You are the most important thing' and this will create feelings of security and reassurance within the child from an early age. It takes practice to interpret the various communication signals that a baby sends out and it is natural that it will take time for a parent to connect with their baby. However, ignoring a baby's cries because of other duties or an inability to deal with the situation is not an effective parenting style and will ultimately create an insecure baby as well as a stressed parent.

It also helps to view a baby as a little person in your home that you engage with on an ongoing basis rather than just something to attend to at feeding or changing time. Babies will love being spoken to, having the Qur'an recited to them or simply just being in your company. They love you unconditionally and want to spend meaningful time with you; they do not want to feel like they are a burden. Let your child know that they are more important than the dishes in the sink or cooking dinner and they will reward you for it.

THE RIGHTS OF A CHILD OVER ITS PARENTS

Every child has the basic right to suckling, sustenance, affection and education from their parents. Islamic civilisation was built and maintained by generations of Muslims who were serious in giving these rights to their children. Deviation from this was not accepted. An incident during the caliphate of Umar ﵁ highlights this.

A man came to the second Caliph with his young son, complaining that his son was disobedient and insolent to his parents. Instead of admonishing the boy 'Umar calmly asked him what the matter was. The boy replied by asking, 'Do I not have rights over my father? Are there not certain things which he should do for me?' 'Umar replied that the child naturally has rights over his parents. When the boy asked to hear some of these, 'Umar said, 'When a man wishes to marry, he should marry a virtuous woman to be the mother of his children. When Allah Almighty blesses him with a child he should give him a pleasant name. He should teach the child Qur'an and Sunnah. When the child reaches the age of maturity, he should arrange for his or her marriage.' The boy was listening quietly and then said, 'My father did none of these for me. As far as my mother is concerned, she belonged to a certain group of immoral people. I do not wish to name these people, but they are known for their illegal sexual relations. When I was born my father named me Khunfasa (black beetle). As a result, wherever I go I am taunted by other children as being a cockroach. My father did not arrange for my Islamic education. I have never attended a mosque or a school, and I have no knowledge of Qur'an or Sunnah.' When the boy had finished his complaint 'Umar turned to the father and said, 'You had severed relations with your son before he severed relations with you.'

GOING BACK TO WORK

The key to the effective parenting of new born babies lies in making a conscious effort to understand the baby. Parents learn this by watching their babies, listening to them and waiting for their reactions. Babies' ranges of signals are limited and they can only communicate with parents if they recognise their signals. Thus, developing loving relationships and forming secure connections with babies is most important, especially for mothers. It would be unfortunate if Muslim women were to shy away from their tasks as mothers before this connection was secure. This would result in their losing the joy of rearing children. Unless absolutely required, Muslim mothers should not let their children be raised by child-minders. In that case, exceptional care should be taken in the choice of the person. We cannot expect our children to grow as Muslims when our young ones spend most of their formative time with those who know very little about Islam and its essence, no matter how professional they may be. Islam has burdened men to earn for the family and give women respite, especially when the children are very young.

> ***The wrong action in not providing maintenance is enough to waste a person's deeds.***
> (Ahmad and Abu Dawud)

If a father finds it really difficult economically to sustain the family during the early years of child-rearing, the mother can step in with part-time or temporary work to help out, if she wishes. However, this needs mutual consultation between husband and wife. In any case, the work and its environment should be decent. It must be kept in mind that rearing children is never inferior to working outside the home for an employer.

Chapter Three

Infancy and the Pre-School Years

If you have a child, then treat him like a child. Play with him like a child and do not impose yourself on him like an adult. (Ibn 'Asakir)

FROM BABY TO TODDLER

As babies grow, the demands on parents change. No sooner do parents learn the delicate art of responding to their demands, such as rocking them to sleep, than they suddenly realise that they have an entirely different creature to contend with – a toddler.

As babies grow in physique and intellect, their world starts widening beyond the world of parents and siblings at home to include more and more people around them. The surrounding environment keeps on imprinting diverse pictures on their memory and helps in building their characters. Every day they master new skills, speak new words and understand new concepts through human interactions, games and other activities. By the time they are sitting and crawling they learn how to make mess of things. Within a year they are used to doing a lot of mischief! They become ever more active and need protection from a lot of household dangers when they walk, run, talk and poke into anything they find interesting. Some children are more inquisitive than others. However, every home with a toddler in it should be made safe. All dangerous items, small or large, should be out of their reach. They should not be left on their own or unsupervised at this time. All parents must learn a few basic rules of first aid and use common sense in times of emergency. It is better to be safe than to be sorry.

This is the time when parents have a tremendous role to play in their child's rapid intellectual development and their spiritual quest. Children take life as an adventure and work on impulse as they are not yet ready to grapple with the thinking process. They play and through this learn various life skills. In order to teach them the reality of life and contain some of their natural impulsive behaviour a number of do's and don'ts may need to be set from childhood. This is important for their safety as well. But too many do's and don'ts can impede their intellectual development. As such, parents need to be sensitive and should only establish those rules that are essential. Even then they should make sure that children continue to learn and that too many rules do not hamper their natural development, creativity and innovative power. Parents should refrain from shouting and frightening, let alone physically punishing them. Children should gradually be led to be able to understand that the basic rules are for their safety, sound development and social acceptability. A verbal comment or appropriate look from parents should be sufficient at this stage of life.

Children are unique. They gradually settle into their characteristic nature. Some are calm and some are restless. Getting to know young children - to 'read' their mind - is relatively easier than getting to know older people, as children are generally expressive and forthcoming. They cannot conceal their feelings and their innocent looks and impulsive actions generally reveal everything about them. Many children cry a lot and want continuous company from someone. Some cannot sleep on their own, as they always need someone at their side. Many children find their way to their mother's bed at night. As every child is different, mothers often have to adapt and sacrifice their comfort.

The importance of physical closeness between a mother and her child in the early years should not be underestimated. By being 'harsh' to them in this most important phase of life, for example, by forcing them to sleep alone in a room before they are ready, some mothers loosen their precious bond with their children. Muslim parents, especially mothers, need to make sure that their children are emotionally content, and to realise that this will vary from one child to another.

PARENTING STYLES

Conscientious Muslim parents have to deal, on the one hand, with their children's immediate demands and, on the other, their balanced growth so that they develop as good human beings. By investing time, energy and attention in the early years of the children's lives, parents can reap dividends later. Research has shown that there are broadly three different styles of child-rearing:

i) authoritarian
ii) permissive
iii) authoritative

They generally lead to different types of child behaviour.

■ Authoritarian

In the authoritarian style, parents try to shape and control their children through orders, obedience to authority, work and tradition. Children are judged by how well they conform to standards set by adults. Creativity and personal accomplishments are probably not rejected outright, but have little recognition. This military style of discipline from early childhood has a negative impact on the personality of a child and influences their future behaviour towards other people. This style of parenting saps the joy from childhood and inhibits a child's natural personality. The resulting child may become withdrawn and turn out to be timid and anxious. Shouting at a child or punishing them will certainly create order and discipline in the home at the time, but it will leave the scars of low self-esteem and lack of creativity and self-discipline. Research has found that this style will impact boys more negatively than girls.

Some parents adopt this style in order to fulfil their need to exert power over someone, to control how they want their child to turn out, or as an outlet for their own frustrations. Children are not objects to be used to satisfy anyone's ego, or robots that can be ordered to conform to their parents' wishes. Children are human beings that need to be allowed to develop their personalities, albeit within boundaries. But those boundaries need to be imposed with kindness and flexibility not harshness and rigidity.

■ Permissive

The other extreme is the permissive style, in which parents give in to their children's impulses and actions. Permissive parents do not make any demands on their children nor impose any form of discipline or authority, in other words, the household is ruled by the child.

This is tantamount to an abuse of the parent-child relationship. It is the duty of parents to guide and nurture their children into the best human beings that they can be based on their greater life experience. To hand over the reins of this responsibility to the children themselves is irresponsible and neglectful. As a result, these children tend to be immature and self-centred. They generally find it hard to cope with social responsibility and independence.

Some parents adopt this style because of the lack of confidence in their own parenting ability or because they fear the displeasure of their children if they subject them to discipline. Again this stems from a misunderstanding of the parental role. Children may momentarily show you their pleasure if you submit to their demands, but a parent can only command respect and love if they act as a parent, guide and mentor.

■ Authoritative

This is the middle-of-the-road and balanced way of parenting, in which the parent is the figure of authority and children work within the boundaries that the parents have defined. Where this differs from the authoritarian style is in the way in which parents assert their authority. This parenting style depends on open and loving communication between parents and children, consultation, flexibility and accommodation. Authoritative parents guide their children in a rational manner without bullying them, they explain their decisions rather than imposing them and engage with their children rather than shouting at them. Children are allowed the space and freedom in which to express their personalities and individuality, but they do so in a way which is respectful and pleasing to their parents.

Children brought up in this style are generally happy and self-reliant and grow up with the ability to meet the challenges of life. They become socially responsible, dynamic and friendly. These children are a pleasure to raise and an asset to their parents.

> ***'The believer (mumin) is the mirror of another believer (mumin)...'*** (Abu Dawud)

Parents are genuinely their children's mirrors. By carefully observing the parents, a child can realise how much affection, respect and trust parents possess. If they feel contented and valued, children will grow confidently as good human beings.

THE FORMATIVE PERIOD

A child's reasoning ability starts developing from the age of twelve months. They are driven towards acquiring practical skills, such as putting on shoes and learning to walk. They also learn how to communicate orally and are busy in exploring the world around them. It is a physically demanding stage for parents as they have to be constantly aware of their child's safety and well-being while allowing them to indulge their natural curiosity.

The parent-child relationship is dynamic and reciprocal, but in the early years, it is the parents' job to build the foundations for a strong relationship. Parents do not have to be psychologists or expert educationalists to rear their toddlers. What they need is common sense and an elementary understanding of human behaviour to interact with their children and contribute to the latter's development. Understanding the stages of the child's physical, intellectual and emotional development helps in making appropriate demands on children. With the passage of time, children's skills and understanding of the world expand. They learn how to relate to other people and develop life habits.

The formative years of a child's life are spent in playing. Running, chasing, climbing, jumping, throwing and other physical activities develop their bodies and help their motor coordination. While doing all this they talk and talk. All children are different, and it is interesting that boys and girls play differently from an early age. Generally, boys play outside in larger groups and physically tough games, often in order to dominate others. On the other hand, girls generally play gentler indoor games. This natural inclination is amazing. However trivial the games may seem, it is actually through play that children learn about the world around them and their ideas of acceptable social interaction are formed. Physical activities enhance self-esteem and confidence, while intellectually stimulating games help a child's creativity and confidence. It is, therefore, important to allow children plenty of time to play, preferably in fresh air. The Prophet Muhammad ﷺ was exemplary in giving importance to physical activities and fun. Even when older, he himself used to engage in innocent play with his young wife, A'ishah, may Allah be pleased with her, and showed interest in children's play.

Children grow in size and shape rapidly. They grow in intellect; their brain develops faster than any other organ. Scientists have found that by the age of five, a child's brain reaches nine-tenths of an adult brain, although their body is still one third of adult weight. This is the best age for memorising the Qur'an by heart. Many pioneering Muslim scholars, natural and social scientists became *huffadh* (memorisers of the Qur'an) in their early years.

While memorisation is a useful skill, arguably the most important life skill that a child can possess is the ability to think. Most importantly, they need to learn how to think creatively and with open minds; as the proverb goes, 'Your mind is like a parachute. It only works if it is open.' Creative thinking within individuals leads to a productive and dynamic society in which everyone can fulfil their potential. Many parents are afraid of allowing their children to be truly creative, in the mistaken belief that they will lose control of their children or that open-mindedness and creativity are incompatible with Islam. Nothing could be further from the truth. Creative thinking is about challenging the child's mind and expanding their horizons, allowing them to 'think outside the box', make new connections and come up with innovative ideas. A few examples of how this can be achieved from an early age are:

- Do puzzles and games that challenge the mind.
- Visit new places. This can be a different area of your own neighbourhood or a different country. Get your child to think about the differences and similarities.
- Encourage them to think differently about routine activities. For example, if you regularly go to the park, ask your child how they would design a climbing frame. Allow your child to be creative (safely) in the kitchen.
- Write imaginative stories with made-up characters and situations.
- Read a variety of books that feed the imagination.
- Have plenty of conversations about the day's events, feelings and thoughts.

It is amazing that in such a short space of time, a baby has grown from a helpless being into a little person that is able to think in words and symbols, relate them to daily life, learn languages, commit to memory and develop the capacity for logical thinking. Throughout this time, there are a few basic principles to bear in mind whether you have a new born, infant or toddler:

■ Invest Time in Your Child

Parents need to spend quality time with their children in order to understand them and teach them life skills. This is above and beyond the time that parents spend in dealing and fulfilling their children's short-term physical needs. It is a two-way process in which parents communicate in an age-appropriate manner with their children while enriching their own knowledge and experience. All children are born with innate potential, parents need only to help them blossom to their fullest at the time that is right for that child. However, you need to spend time with your child in order to recognise what their particular strengths are and which areas need your support. There are considerable demands on parents' time, but the astute parent realises that quality time invested in children yields the greatest rewards in this life and the next.

■ Understand Your Child

There is mercy in the differences that Allah has created, and the world is beautiful because it is inhabited by human beings with singular personalities. Children are different in temperaments and they may grow up with personalities different from their parents and siblings. It is important that they feel confident in expressing their individuality and celebrating their differences. Children are not meant to be clones of their parents.

■ Empathise with Your Child

In order to raise children effectively, Muslim parents must learn to empathise with them. The power of entering into another's feelings and undergoing their experiences with creative imagination is an important skill. The most effective trainers of human beings, the prophets, were successful in this technique. By trying to put themselves in their children's position, parents can understand the nature of their needs and learn to see their rapidly changing and enlarging world. Empathy tells parents that children's day-to-day life, like everybody else's, is driven by love, fear, self-interest and other human instincts. Through empathy and insight parents can build their children's sense of worth and encourage their involvement in decisions concerning their lives. This sets good examples for the child who, in turn, learns how to empathise with others in life.

■ Respect Your Child

It may seem trivial, but it is important to treat your child with respect. They are not objects to be dragged along behind their parents like a suitcase or inferior beings that can be spoken to, or about, disrespectfully. As adults, we expect a certain amount of respect from other adults, but we sometimes forget to extend this respect to our children. Some parents simply communicate with their children by issuing a string of orders, without saying 'please' and 'thank you'. Some parents refer to children as 'Shaytans' when they act up. Children will learn respect when they are treated as such, when they are spoken to kindly, when they are spoken about with dignity. They will appreciate it when an adult takes the time to explain things to them. For example, if you are going to attend a wedding, then take five minutes to explain to your baby or child, where the family is going, how long it will take and why it is important. This level of respect will be rewarded with respect.

THE NEED FOR BALANCED DEVELOPMENT

As parents, we wish to give our children the best start in life and we may do this by setting up trust funds, paying for private education or buying them things that we did not have ourselves as children. However, the best thing we can do for our children is to give them the tools they need to be a success in this world and the Hereafter; the inner resources they need to acquire peace of mind and heart.

This requires that parents pay attention to their children's physical, intellectual, emotional, spiritual and social development. It is only when parents attend to ALL of these areas that they can expect the result to be in a well-rounded confident and dynamic individual with a holistic outlook to life and a balanced approach between this world and the

Hereafter. We cannot always shield our children from life's problems, from being hurt or disappointed. We cannot always be there to pick up the pieces, as much as we would like to be. However, we can rest in the knowledge that we have given them the skills that they need to cope with life.

As children grow under the care of parents and other adults, they develop personalities that are unique to them. Some traits are inherited, others are acquired, which raises the question of nature versus nurture. While this is the subject of great debate, it should not have a bearing on the issue of rearing children through positive parenting, or else the whole purpose of education is rendered meaningless. While genetic influence has an effect on child's life, environmental contribution is hugely important. A child's upbringing, health care, education, abundance or deficiency of love, family manners - all influence their development and mould their personalities. In the end, parents should concentrate on what they can potentially achieve through their best efforts and leave the rest in Allah's hands; in other words a balance between positive action and *tawakkul.*

In the post-modern industrialised world, where Muslim children are growing in material abundance, the predominant culture is one of individualism, distrust of authority and rebellion. Indulgence and permissiveness are norms. The lack of family discipline and absence of strong moral codes have led to sexual experimentation, drug culture, violence and confusion in gender roles. Electronic media have globalised this permissiveness and brought it into our own homes.

It may seem premature to think about these social issues as a parent of a baby, but the reality is that this is the society which our children will grow up in. In such circumstances, Muslim parents can neither insulate their children from society completely nor allow their children to swim in this sea of *jahiliyyah*. The best path is to guide our children through this sea when they are young and to equip them with the life skills they need to negotiate it for themselves when they are older. The following points are helpful in achieving a balanced child.

- ***Instil Islamic Spirit Right From the Start***

The most effective way to survive modern negative trends is to instil a deep sense of Islamic spirit in children right from the start of their lives. Children generally utter their first meaningful words when they are about a year old. Between one to two years the average child learns about two hundred words. Development is faster after two years when they can connect words and develop thinking skills. Language development is enhanced when adults around keep on talking to their infants in baby-talk, not normal speech. Parents should talk to them in meaningful and short sentences with good rhythm. Reading good nursery rhymes and telling short stories and family incidents with verbal and body expression delight children and make them interested in learning.

It is obvious that children will absorb the vocabulary that they hear most often around them in natural speech. So if the adults greet each other with salaam and scatter their speech with *insha'Allah*, *masha Allah* and *alhamdulillah*, for example, then children will naturally repeat these phrases in the correct context without the need to be taught. Similarly, if the daily routine of a family involves *salah*, recitation of the Qur'an and *dhikr*, then again the child will subconsciously internalise the importance of these actions.

It is essential for parents to read age appropriate books to babies and children regularly. This will open horizons and instil a life-long love of reading and learning in them. As well as general story books, there are a number of excellent Islamic children's books on the market that make wonderful reading. Islamic books do not just have to be about the Prophets or incidents in Islamic history. There are a number of story books that simply have Muslim characters and situations that a child may be more familiar in identifying with.

• *But Mind Your Child's Maturity Level...*

Some parents, through lack of experience, can be a little too over-zealous in trying to instil elements of the *deen* in their children. Like all other life skills, understanding of the *deen* also develops with time and must be fed to a child gently but continually and in a manner that is appropriate to that child's age and comprehension.

When recounting the stories of the Prophets or other factual events, it is important that parents clarify that these are real and serious events, not just make-believe. A great deal of the children's entertainment market today relies on fairy-tales, fictional characters and celebrities, that it is important that we make this distinction in their minds.

On the other hand, certain aspects of the *deen* should not be made to seem overwhelming to children when it is beyond their capability to grasp certain concepts. For example, some parents use the tactic of frightening their children into behaving or complying with references to Allah, His anger, His punishment or bad deeds being recorded. This builds up a mental picture in the child of Allah as a vengeful, punishing Being to be feared. The young heart and mind will be more receptive when it is taught with love and kindness rather than fear and shame.

• *Manners and Habits*

> ***No father can give his child a better gift than good manners, good character and good education.***
> (at-Tirmidhi)

Teaching children Islam is not limited to teaching them of the rituals and rules of the religion. It would be an incomplete education that taught a child the do's and don'ts of *fiqh* or the perfection of the pronunciation of their Qur'an, without instilling Islamic character in them, for Islam is about character. The Prophet Muhammad ﷺ was sent to perfect character and was the embodiment of good manners and nobility.

In order to create a generation that is among the best of human beings, that enjoins the good and forbids the evil, we must embody within our children the highest of values and morals so that, as proud young Muslims, they can differentiate between good and bad. We must try to infuse in them a sound knowledge of Islam and contemporary society from the beginning so that in future, as adolescents and adults, they do not run away from society but interact, engage and contribute to it without compromising their principles. This is important for the future of Muslims, not only in the West but everywhere in the world.

Values and morals encompass a vast range of behaviours and characteristics, from simply saying 'please' and 'thank you' right through to unswerving patience and gratitude in times of extreme adversity. A noble character is formed from the traits of humility, purity of speech, tolerance, patience, gratitude, compassion, and manifests itself through actions and speech that do not harm or hurt other people. The noble character is generous and giving of itself in service to others, even in times of personal hardship. It is well worth reading a biography of the Prophet ﷺ from the point of view of his character, in order to appreciate just how exemplary his conduct was. We need to aspire to this level of *adab* within our own personal lives and within our homes, so that our children have good examples to emulate.

As mentioned earlier, the education process should start from the later days of conception. However, the early years (birth up to five or seven years) are especially significant for children. At this stage, they are highly impressionable and absorb whatever messages are around them. This has a long-lasting impact on their brain. Imparting education is a gradual and natural process, but should not be done in a coercive manner. It is also most effective when learnt by example rather than in theory only. If children are taught one thing but see their parent behaving in another, then children are likely to grow in a state of confusion. However, education and training are pro-active processes. Good human qualities flourish with effort and support from good people. Islam, as a comprehensive *deen*, has guidelines on all aspects of life. Children can only know them with adult help, so that they can practise what is good and stay away from what is unacceptable. Continuous training by effective trainers - fathers and mothers - is the best way to produce results. The parents' role is to help and guide sensitively and consistently. Overburdening a child out of religious fervour can be detrimental to their spiritual well-being. Parents need to bear their child's age and maturity level in mind before they demand high standards from them.

• ***Reward, Discipline and Self-esteem***

As children become more socially skilled, they develop self-awareness. It is at this stage that the valid concept of good and bad needs to be inculcated in them. Success and failure affect them to the extent that they sometimes become overconfident and at other times confused and despondent. Parents need to buffer their children from these emotional highs and lows, by being calm, dependable and understanding, and ensuring that their child remains assured and contented.

Young children are like 'raw materials'. Parents and elders help make them a good 'product'. As children learn from their surroundings they need consistent good discipline. This means teaching children how to behave sensibly and responsibly. Parental responsibility is to educate them in a way that they feel good when they behave well and feel bad when they do not. If this can be inculcated in them from within, that will remain embedded in them for the rest of their life. There is a mistaken belief in some cultures that the only way to discipline children is by telling off or punishing them. Sanctions used to discipline a child need to be used with proper judgement, consistency and fairness. It is vital for parents to make sure both of them give the same message when dealing with or disciplining their child. Different treatment from fathers and mothers confuse children and can prove disastrous.

The most severe penalty for children is parental disapproval. Children need to know why they are being disciplined so that they feel that their parents do not dislike them and discipline is just for correcting their inappropriate behaviour. Once disciplined for some genuine reason, the child does not need to carry the guilt. Punishment should only be used for destructive or serious misbehaviour otherwise it may miss its objective. Nobody wants children to be defiant in the end. Crude punishment may stop children temporarily from doing something wrong, but it does not teach them how to overcome the behaviour issue. Physical punishment, such as spanking, may not be illegal but it has to be used in the proper context and only with the purpose of educating the child. Indiscriminate or inconsistent punishment takes away children's fear and can make them rebellious at a later stage. Shaming or belittling them, especially in public, does not help their self-esteem. The maxim, 'love in public, correct in private', is very important. Children must feel that their parents still love them even after the punishment.

Parents feel proud when their children achieve a success, however small it might be. It is essential parents express their feelings directly and openly about their children's accomplishments. Genuine recognition increases self-esteem. Children need natural praise and acknowledgement from their parents and elders to make them feel good about themselves and reinforce their confidence and enhance their abilities.

At the same time, shortcomings should not be seen as the end of the world. 'Never mind, if you work harder, you will do better next time, insha'Allah', is a type of sincere comment and encouragement from parents that can help maintain children's self-esteem. Destroying someone else's self-confidence is easy: a simple negative look or apparently trivial comment is enough to lower it.

Children take to heart every word that adults say to them, even though the adult may have uttered those words in jest. Parents must be mindful in the manner in which they praise or discipline children; using a tone of voice and words that are not over the top. If children do something very silly, the best way to deal with it is not the punishment or threat of it, but to make them realise that doing wrong is in itself upsetting and bad for them.

A common mistake is for some parents to overlook good behaviour or take it for granted while disciplining a child for their bad behaviour. Giving a child attention (even if it is negative) only when they behave badly, serves to reinforce the child's bad behaviour. The magical way to reduce behavioural problems is to recognise, praise and encourage children's good behaviour consistently. Examples of times when praise is warranted are when the child shows: honesty, integrity, respect, courtesy, consideration for others and so on.

The golden rules of discipline are to:

- use judgement as to whether praise or sanction is necessary;
- praise or sanction at appropriate times;
- be diligent and consistent in praising;
- make sure your praise or sanction is genuine, not over-the-top;
- maintain the level of discipline according to the weight of the action;
- make sure children know why they are praised or disciplined;
- observe whether praise or discipline is working;
- never stop giving love to the child, even after discipline.

THE ISSUES AT THIS AGE

■ Toilet-training and General Cleanliness

The concept of *taharah* (cleanliness) is very important in Islam and is a prerequisite for performing *salah*. Parents should be diligent about children's physical cleanliness from birth. In this regard, it is better to wash a child when changing their nappy rather than simply wiping them with a baby wipe.

When a toddler has reached a certain level of maturity, in communication and body coordination, then the process of toilet training can begin. It is vital that the child is ready, physically and mentally, to undergo this process, otherwise it is frustrating and time-consuming for both the parent and the child. There are a number of books that will outline a variety of methods that can be used to train a child. However, the key to all of these is patience and consistency in seeing the process through to its conclusion. It is a great change for the child and a milestone in their independence. Parents must empathise that, while some children welcome change, others may be more reluctant. There will be accidents and periods of apparent regression, but these are all part of the process, however frustrating they may be. The successful parent will be prepared for this and help their child through the process with love and hard work, without taking their frustrations out on the child.

■ Food

The adage, 'You are what you eat' is very true and parents need to be mindful from birth about what their child eats and drinks. Not only should this be halal, but should also be *tayyab* (pure) and nutritious. There is now clear labelling on products and access to a wider variety of halal foods than ever before. As children grow, the concept of halal and haram should be embedded within them.

Pre-prepared foods may be convenient to use during busy periods, but there is much benefit in preparing meals at home from fresh, wholesome ingredients. It is also very beneficial if the whole family can sit together for at least one meal a day and share their experiences of the day. This will instil table manners and food etiquette in children and also provides quality bonding time for the family that should ideally last throughout their childhood. Children who may be fussy or slow eaters by themselves may benefit from a group setting where they are encouraged to behave and eat as everyone else, particularly if there are siblings.

■ Coping with Frustration and Tantrums

Toddlers go through an enormous amount of change and growth in a short space of time. There is still much in the world that they cannot understand and they are not quite fully skilled in articulating their emotions. When events frustrate, disappoint or anger them, then the result can be a full-blown tantrum!

Dealing with tantrums requires a two-pronged approach, both of which should be used in parallel. The first step is to prevent the factors that cause a tantrum in the first place. Children who are consistently loved, cared for and whose genuine needs are met are emotionally contented. They are far less likely to throw a tantrum in the first place. Steps to prevent a tantrum would include: ensuring that the child is well-fed, hydrated, not over-tired, not bored or over-stimulated or frightened. Children also learn how to behave in response to emotions from their parents. If parents set a bad example to children, exhibit emotional outbursts and raise their voices, then the child is more likely to behave in this fashion. Lack of patience, tolerance and steadfastness all have a negative effect on children, firstly, by frightening them and secondly by sending them the wrong message about how to deal with emotions. The calm and patient parents are more likely to breed calm and patient children.

However, life is not ideal and all children will throw tantrums at some stage in their early years. There is always a build-up before the tantrum, which the perceptive parent will be able to spot. A child may not behave in their usual manner, for example, they may be more disruptive or vocal than usual. This is the point at which parents need to intervene – when they see this tension building up within their child. Sometimes a hug and reassurance works wonders.

Once a tantrum is in full swing, then the best thing a parent can do is to remain calm themselves. Getting angry simply adds more emotion to an already charged emotional situation. According to the age and maturity of the child and the circumstances, the parent can either take the child away from the situation and distract them, or acknowledge it and allow them to disperse their pent-up emotion in a controlled fashion.

Children undergo a spectrum of emotions on a daily basis and so it is also a good idea to incorporate techniques in everyday life that will act as a regular release for emotions. These include:

- reading stories to children with characters that experience emotion and discussing these with the child;
- allowing the child to draw or paint scenes or thoughts that may be troubling them;
- sport and outdoor play is a good way of releasing aggression;
- martial arts is beneficial in calming and controlling emotions.

Use of the TV and Computer

The struggle for survival in the real world keeps parents very busy. The pressure of day-to-day jobs or businesses and the need for extra money to top up family income and meet other social demands, strains them. Time becomes a rare commodity and, as a result, quality time with children suffers. In situations like these, TV can unwittingly take on the role of a convenient baby-sitter. Some parents believe that children's TV is largely harmless fun that keeps children quiet for a few hours.

However, even children's programmes may show inappropriately dressed people, permissiveness of pop music and dancing, disrespect of elders and wasting of food, to name a few. Over time these silently corrode the values and ethos that Muslim parents have worked so hard to instil.

TV is regarded essential by most and it is very influential on our lifestyles; it influences our opinions, provides common talking points and moulds our personalities. TV may serve some useful purpose for children as entertainment and learning, but this should be a limited and vetted amount in an otherwise varied schedule.

Young children of busy parents may be watching several hours of TV a day. This keeps them from interacting with others, using their imagination and creativity, stagnates their minds and limits their concentration. In addition, it leaves them more tense and may cause eye strain and other health issues.

Children are naturally physically active and sociable. They would rather play and be in the company of other people. Research has found that many children watch TV because they have nothing else to do, or when they feel bored. Parents should plan their schedules between themselves to make time for their little ones and engage their children in creative activity. This requires a little thought and imagination, but does not mean that parents have to abandon all their other tasks. Little children are just as happy sitting in the kitchen watching their mother cook or playing with spoons and saucepans. Older children will be happy drawing or painting on the kitchen table or even helping Mum with some simple and safe tasks.

A similar argument can be used for computers, tablets and smartphones with their ever increasing games and apps. At social functions, such as weddings, it is now common to see young children staring at their individual screens without noticing anyone or anything around them. How will our children learn to mix with their elders or converse with others? How will they learn to be a member of wider society if they do not know social graces and etiquettes? These devices may have their limited place in the Muslim home for educational purposes but they are not substitutes for human interaction.

PRE-SCHOOL CHILDCARE OPTIONS

Most countries do not require children to be in full-time education until they are five or six years old, although there are a number of options for childcare from birth until this age.

A couple must discuss between themselves whether or not one parent, usually the mother, is able to stay at home with her child until the child is ready to go to school. This would be the ideal scenario. Children are our greatest assets and we need to treat them as such. They are born physically, emotionally, socially, mentally and spiritually dependent on their parents. This is a huge responsibility for any parent to fulfil. Like a sculptor, the parent must take the delicate raw material and carefully coax and soothe and shape it into a thing of beauty. This requires time and effort.

Parents who stay at home to look after their young ones are not expected to have formal syllabuses but conscientious parents have targets that they focus on in educating their children at home from a very young age. They set goals for their children that are age- and personality- appropriate and endeavour to make the home a loving nursery and pre-school. The child benefits from having a carer that loves them more than anyone else in the world and tailor-made goals and targets achieved in a setting that is a safe and loving home. For a broader experience and greater social interaction, the stay-at-home parent can supplement their efforts at home with outings to play groups and activities.

As a child nears three and four years of age, parents may feel that the child would benefit from a more formal educational setting and thus may choose to send them to a nursery or pre-school place for a few sessions in the week. This will help the child settle into the school routine with more ease.

Mothers that worked full-time outside the home prior to having children may feel frustrated at the lack of intellectual stimulation and social life on becoming a stay-at-home mother. They may also feel the loss of their own income and the independence that goes with it. These are all valid and normal feelings. However, motherhood is an honour and a privilege. It is not bestowed to everyone and the early years of a child's life pass very quickly. The mother can return to full-time work when the child goes to school.

The arrival of a child does bring additional financial pressures with it. Islam has placed the responsibility of providing for the family on the man. As far as possible, it is ideal when this is the case, so the mother can stay at home and look after the children. It may not be possible to afford some of the luxuries of life during this time, but children will benefit more from a simpler life with a stay-at-home parent. The latest gadgets, cupboards full of clothes and toys, and foreign holidays do not make up for absent parents.

It may be that there is no other option except that both parents have to work in order to ensure a basic standard of living for the family. In this case, there are a few options that can be explored in order to minimise the negative effects on children. It may be possible that one of the parents can work part-time or that both parents can work flexibly in order for there to be a parent at home some of the time. It is worth talking to members of the extended family such as aunts and grandparents, or friends, who may be able to offer childcare in a wholesome and Islamic environment.

It should be considered a last resort to leave babies and very young children in institutions for several hours of the day. However professionally run these centres are, they are not an adequate replacement for a loving mother in an Islamic home. Nevertheless, if this is the only option, then the parents should make the effort to give quality, undiluted time to their children when they are at home.

Chapter Four

Primary School Years

"When a man makes up a story for his child, he becomes a father and a child together, listening." (Rumi)

The primary school years are taken to mean the first years of formal school education usually from the ages of between five and eleven. The purpose of a primary school is to provide the foundation of formal education and to impart basic skills in literacy, numeracy, communication and social interaction.

CHOOSING A PRIMARY SCHOOL

The choice of how parents elect to have their child educated at this age will have a knock-on effect on their future education, so this is a decision that should not be taken lightly nor delayed unnecessarily. There are four broad options at this stage:

- Local state-run school
- Private school
- Islamic school
- Home schooling

The first place to look is within the locality for schools that are close to home. Indeed some state schools will only accept children who live within a certain distance from the school, in other words, within the catchment area. Parents have been known to move to a different area if the schools in their own local area are under-performing. If this is the case, such a decision needs to be made well in advance.

Schools often produce prospectuses or have websites that parents can browse. While they are designed to present the best side of the school, they can offer an insight as to the breadth of subjects taught and the extra-curricular activities and opportunities offered. All schools must follow some curriculum guidelines that are set by the government and children must attain certain levels in assessments that take place periodically. Many schools make these results available in the form of league tables that display the percentage of children that have achieved a certain standard in literacy and numeracy. Finally, it is worth looking to see where primary school leavers go on and attend secondary school. Schools may also be subject to independent inspection and regulatory visits and, again, these detailed reports can be found on the internet.

There is no substitute, however, to actually visiting a school during a typical school day, seeing the pupils and teachers at work in the environment in which your child will potentially spend around seven hours a day. It is worth considering: the class sizes and demographic of the pupils; the feel of the classrooms and recreational spaces; the enthusiasm of the teachers; the behaviour of the pupils; the school's attitude towards teaching and discipline and so on.

Private schools are an expensive option. However, they are known for providing an excellent academic education, good range of extra-curricular activities, high teacher-pupil ratios, strong discipline and good resources. It is up to parents to decide whether the expense is justifiable.

It is undeniable that, however academically excellent, the ethos of a school in the West is liberal and permissive. Many schools teach Religious Education as well as Sex Education, even at this tender age. Unfortunately, many Muslim parents are unaware that there is a provision under which they can withdraw their children from these lessons.

Nevertheless, some parents feel that it is not possible for their young ones to grow and develop within the spirit of Islam in a mainstream Western school and fear that their Muslim identity would be diluted or compromised. In this case, an Islamic school would certainly provide a wholesome environment for a young person to be strongly anchored in the *deen*.

There is no one 'best' school. A parent's job is to have understood the nature of their child, consider their own priorities in terms of formal education and then to select an institution in which the child will flourish and which will fulfil most of the parents' expectations. One school may provide an excellent academic education but lack warmth and nurturing; another may offer a smaller range of subjects but provide strong moral guidance and loving discipline. It is a case of working out where your 'plant' will flourish.

In some cases, parents may not have access to private or Islamic schools and the local state-schools may not be suitable. In this case, many countries give parents the right to educate their children at home, provided that they fulfil certain criteria. While this option requires a great deal of parental motivation and dedication, it also gives the parent complete control over what their child is exposed to and provides an education that is tailor-made for the child.

In summary, the following points are useful in looking at a prospective school:

- Is private school an affordable option?
- Which schools are in the catchment area?
- What is the ethos or culture of the school like?
- What is the demographic of the school's pupils?
- What are the attitudes and behaviour of the pupils like?
- What are the attitudes of the teaching and non-teaching staff?
- What are the facilities like?
- What do the inspection reports, current pupils and their parents say about the school?
- How good are its extra-curricular activities?
- Do you think your child will fit in here?

SCHOOL EXPOSURE

Starting school is an exciting experience for young children and a big responsibility for parents. It is the beginning of their child's independent life. Those who had the advantage of sending their children to pre-school nurseries or playgroups before the statutory school-going age have already passed that step. Their children should have already learnt something about coping in the classroom through listening and responding to adults who are not their parents.

School introduces children to a wide circle of friends and learning opportunities. Some children relish the opportunity and challenges of starting school and the transition from home to school is a smooth and seamless one. Most children, however, do need some time to settle into the demands of a formal, structured school day, away from their parents and home environment for several hours. They may not be able to articulate their fears and anxieties about being taken out of their comfort zone and this may manifest itself as a change in behaviour. There may be more tears, clinging, aggression, introversion or regression to a more childish behaviour, such as thumb sucking or bed wetting.

No parent likes to see their child unhappy, and so this can be a very stressful time. The child should not be punished or shouted at for their change in behaviour as this would be counterproductive. It would be prudent to speak to the school and come up with strategies that will help the child settle. This may be as simple as allowing the child to bring in a favourite toy to school as something familiar to play with. With care and sensitivity, this phase will pass quickly, insha'Allah.

ISSUES IN PRIMARY SCHOOL

There are a number of common issues that primary-school age children experience. Some of these may stem from school while others are home-based. The sensitive parent will learn to pick up these problems early on before they escalate by listening to their child's concerns and noting any unusual or out of character behaviour.

■ Fear of School

The fear of new things is inherent in human nature. Children have common fears, some of them are short-lived, but at times, they cause parents to worry. Some children refuse to go to school for no apparent reason and can go to great lengths to try to avoid it. Parents need to ascertain whether this is because of an unfounded fear or phobia or whether this is due to some physical or medical reason. Some children simply suffer from anxiety when separated from their mothers. Discovering the actual reason will take time and patience, as many children cannot express themselves articulately at an early age. Whatever the reasons, parents should try to empathise with them, try to identify the cause and implement solutions, in partnership with the teachers, with plenty of love and reassurance.

■ Bullying

Some children are loud, noisy and boisterous, especially in the playground; some are hyperactive and others are recluses. Some can be aggressive, giving rise to bullying. Bullying can be carried out by an individual or a group of children on vulnerable children, who are unable or afraid to defend themselves. It can be verbal, psychological or physical. Children being bullied may be unwilling to go to school and even talk to adults. Parents have to keep an eye out for the warning signs and if it ever comes to their attention, they should take this up with the school. It is the responsibility of the school to keep all their children physically, mentally and emotionally safe while in their care. Additionally, it may also be helpful to give the bullied child some skills with which to cope with such situations. These can include assertiveness training or martial arts classes.

■ Birthday Parties and Celebrations

Birthdays are one of the most important cultural aspects of Western family and social life. From the first birthday onwards families, nurseries and primary schools arrange some sort of party on each birthday accompanied by cakes, candles and presents. In fact, birthdays are becoming ever more lavish with expensive venue hire, themes and planners. This seems to be a wasteful extravagance. Birthdays are not part of Muslim culture and are not to be celebrated in the same way that the non-Muslims celebrate their birthdays.

Nevertheless, a parent will never forget the day that their child was born and may wish to mark the occasion as such. If this is the case, then the most dignified way to do this is by using this day to reflect, to seek Allah's forgiveness and to make resolutions for a better future, perhaps accompanied by a special family meal. A family may wish to express their gratitude to Allah by offering extra *nafl* prayers or giving *sadaqah*.

Of course, the issue of attending the birthday parties of other children will arise. Muslim parents need to use their own judgement as to whether they find this fits in with the ethos and values they are teaching their child at home. Many birthday parties will have music, free mixing and dancing and may be an inappropriate environment for the child.

Christmas, Valentine's day, Halloween and so on, may be celebrated in many schools as neutral and innocent fun, but Muslims parents should know that some of them have pagan roots. These festivals are mainly to do with commercialisation and the essence of them has largely been lost. Children may be asked to participate in concerts and parties as a means of celebration. It is expected that, on the part of the school, these activities will be carried out with the cultural and religious sensitivity of all children in mind. However, parents can always voice any concerns they have with the school and come to a mutual agreement about the extent that they are prepared for their child to participate.

■ Self-esteem

Self-esteem and the feeling of self-worth are vital in everybody's lives. They give rise to the inner drive which is essential for one's success in life. Lack or loss of self-esteem is detrimental to the development of children into balanced and achieving adults. As they pass through their primary school phase, they develop an array of personal and social skills, which are drawn from within their school, peer-group, society and families. When they succeed in managing the demands of day-to-day life, they feel confident and this in turn enhances their self-esteem.

Parents are in a unique position to contribute to the development of children's positive self-image. Every time a parent or an adult praises them, cuddles, smiles at and recognises their achievement, their self-esteem is enhanced. On the other hand, a negative or dismissive and uncomplimentary remark or look reduces their self-esteem. Abundant, explicit and loving approval of children makes them self-confident.

Some young children can be very shy and this can be taken as lack of self-esteem. Shyness has two aspects - modesty and self-centredness. Modesty is not only acceptable in Islam, but strongly encouraged. On the other hand, self-centredness is the opposite of self-confidence. A Muslim should never be self-centred. Young children lacking in self-esteem also suffer from 'dependency syndrome.' They need to achieve gradual independence of their parents as they grow, according to that which is age appropriate.

■ Behavioural Issues

Children want to feel loved and accepted by all and are sensitive to the behaviour and words of the people around them. If for some reason, they feel their parents or teachers do not value them, they feel rejected. Parents that continually argue with each other, a depressed parent and other difficult household situations put tremendous pressure on children. Children wrongly believe that they are the cause of the problem and feel guilty and helpless. Some children will 'act out' and express themselves through misbehaviour, breaking rules and adopting other techniques for seeking attention. On the contrary, some children may decide to 'act in' through social withdrawal, depression and losing interest in childlike activities. The reaction could be mild or even severe. While acting-out, children draw attention from everyone around them, but acting-in children suffer in silence, on their own.

Parents and teachers need to be sensitive to changes in a child's normal behaviour pattern and address the fact that it may be linked to a change in the home or school environment. They then need to reassure the child that it is not their fault and be patient in coaxing the child out of their adopted behavioural pattern. When a child feels that they are being listened to and their issues are being addressed by the adults that they trust, then they are less likely to resort to extremes in behaviour.

■ The Challenge with a Gifted or Talented Child

As children grow, their natural abilities become clearer. Are they gifted or talented? Are they bored easily and in need of extra stimulation? Parents might feel proud about having gifted or talented children, but raising them can be very demanding. Not all gifted or talented children are socially and intellectually mature. Here lies the difficulty. In the temptation to achieve brilliant results for their children at an early age many parents forget their emotional and psychological needs. They forget their role of preparing them socially and intellectually, in a holistic way. Children may be very intelligent, but that does not mean that they should be pushed hard to achieve miracles. If Allah blesses some parents with gifted children, they should plan how best this gift can be utilised for their own benefit and the benefit of others.

Over-zealous parents that pressure their children to achieve for glory or to feel superior over others are in fact playing with their children's childhood. Success in a Muslim life is not confined to academic brilliance alone; it depends on whether they can explore their potential and how they use it for the benefit of their community and human beings in general. An example of this is the widely publicised story of Sufiah Yusof, the child prodigy at Oxford University in the late 1990's and her subsequent troubles through life. Arguably she was subjected to a great deal of pressure and scrutiny from her family and the media at an age where she should have been enjoying her childhood. Educational experts from all spectra now agree that children should not be forced to lose their childhood, no matter how intelligent they are.

■ The Challenge with Learning Difficulties

On the other hand, some children have special educational needs in school for cognitive or other difficulties. Others have physical and emotional issues that hamper their learning.

Teachers and parents need to work in harmony to understand their children and address these issues early on in the child's school life. Over the last few decades, educational systems in most Western countries have successfully addressed the needs of children with learning and behaviour difficulties. Teachers are now more equipped in terms of the pastoral aspects of education. Research has shown that at least one in every five children in Britain will have some form of learning difficulty and these need to be addressed with professional efficiency and sensitivity. Children can face these difficulties for the following reasons:

- Sensory and Physical Impairments – Effective learning goes hand in hand with good physical health. Naturally, some medical conditions, such as hearing or visual impairments, will affect learning.
- Cognitive Difficulties – The largest group of children within the Special Needs category are those who are slow learners. There is a positive link between children's general levels of language development and intellectual ability. Children who find it hard to learn to read have also expressive or receptive language difficulties.
- Emotional and Behavioural Difficulties (EBD) – The term is used in relation to children who have difficulty controlling their behaviour and emotions. Unhappy children will themselves have difficulty with coping in the classroom. They gradually develop low self-esteem and as a result cannot cope with the demands of the curriculum.
- Speech and Language Difficulties – These may arise from an

inability to cope with the structure of language or with the way language is used to communicate. Children may exhibit problems with receptive language (processing the language they hear) and/or expressive language (verbalising their thoughts and feelings).

- Social Aspects – Family and social environments are fundamentally important for the development of children. When they grow up in a positive environment in which they can express themselves openly, they feel comfortable and learn quickly. In inappropriate family and/or social modelling, children grow up with EBD and can enter into adolescence with disaffection.

Having Special Educational Needs (SEN) does not mean that children are unfortunate or incapable. In Allah's design, every human being is different but important. All are subject to being tested according to their abilities. Every human being has been created with distinct strengths and weaknesses. Parents should never undermine their children or compare them with other siblings or their friends. Lack of sensitivity can have a devastating effect on their confidence. If a child displays some of the features of SEN requirements, parents should push for a proper assessment by experts and ask the school for appropriate provision. Teachers and educational psychologists have now adopted remedial services within mainstream school education and these can be every effective in restoring a child's confidence and nurturing their potential.

Unpleasant and Rude Language

Successful indeed are the believers who are humble in their prayers and who shun vain conversation. (Qur'an 23:1-3)

Language is a vital means of communication with other human beings. It manifests one's character. The tongue is the root of expressing oneself and the words we use reveal what kind of people we are. The tongue can be used to bring people nearer to each other and closer to Allah and it can also be used to create hatred among people and drive them away from each other and far from Allah. Muslims should put great emphasis on human decency, in language and behaviour. Language must be meaningful and free from obscenity. Cultured and civilised people are refined in their language and manners as vulgarities lead to disastrous consequences. Language is the mirror of civility and culture; vulgarity in language creeps in when there is a decline in society.

Decent language is essential for maintaining a happy family and social harmony. We should ideally speak to others, including children, in a way in which we would like to be spoken to. Sadly, the influence of modern value-less culture is taking its toll. Sexually explicit and abusive words are now common on the streets, in modern entertainment and in online and they filter down to the playground. Muslim parents should ensure that their children are never exposed to such language within the home through adults, TV or social media. It can be quite alarming when your child comes home from school one day armed with some new vocabulary. They should be told firmly never to repeat such words and why. It is important to nip these matters in the bud before they become a habit.

Muslim parents should not compromise on some basic principles of Islam and Islamic manners. Parents' strong views on language work as a deterrent. No matter how frustrated or angry a Muslim may be, and for whatever reasons, they must learn to control their tongue.

THE IMPORTANCE OF READING

One habit that needs to be instilled in our children from the early years is the love of books and the habit of reading. This is the indicator of success of any nation and the hallmark of a civilisation. A learned and well-read society will not only flourish in its own time but will also leave a positive legacy for the future, as was the case with many Muslim dynasties.

Books, aside from being a source of facts and a tool for formal education, are a source of enjoyment and entertainment, creating a world in which children can lose themselves in their imagination. A good book has the ability to motivate and inspire, challenge thinking and create ambition and aspirations. When we read, we become ever-conscious because we have access to other people's opinions and life experiences, and an insight into their minds and hearts. This is instrumental in shaping our thinking and behaviour and widening our perspective. In short, books should be our life companions and the companions of our young people.

To this end, parents must instil a love reading in their children from an early age and every Muslim home should have books and, if possible, a small library. When children have easy access to a variety of interesting and thought-provoking books, they will read voluntarily and their thoughts can form the basis of many interesting family discussions.

PARENT-SCHOOL PARTNERSHIP

Parents know their own children best, but do not always have the experience to and knowledge to teach them, while teachers do have experience with children and knowledge but cannot know your child in the way that you do. Thus, the education of children is best carried out as a partnership between parents and the school.

It is essential that parents take an interest in what their child is doing at school by asking questions about their day. Some children are more forthcoming and detailed in conversations while others may need more encouragement. Given undivided time and attention, children love to share their school experiences with their parents. Parents should listen with enthusiasm and praise their children's attempts at painting, drawing and writing. Whenever there is an opportunity to attend parent-teacher evenings or classroom viewings, then ideally both parents should avail these times to talk to their child's teacher and see their class work.

If parents feel that there are any other concerns regarding their child's education, well-being or sense of identity, then parents should make an appointment to see the relevant teacher without delay. A constructive flow of communication between home and school is absolutely essential for the child's best interests.

Many schools also allow parental input through surveys, questionnaires, parent engagement groups and even as a school governor. These avenues allow parents to provide constructive comments that will help shape the future of their child's education. It is against the spirit of Islam to sit back and passively express dissatisfaction for an institution. The pro-active parent understands that they themselves are responsible for affecting change if they wish to see it and to be part of the solution.

The first step for parents is to arm themselves with knowledge of the system that their child is in. Parents should be familiar with the educational issues of the day, the school curriculum and a clear understanding of the strengths and weaknesses of their child's school. They should also be confident enough to articulate their views politely yet assertively. Schools are not stagnant places, teaching the same syllabuses decade after decade. They are dynamic institutions that change with the times in response to societal changes and changing government legislations. Schools now, certainly in the big cities, are more sensitive than they were a generation ago to cultural and religious needs. That change has come about because of pro-active voices, but there is still some way to go. By being the pro-active voices of today, parents can ensure the best possible educational outcomes for their own children and grandchildren.

Though formal education in schools may be an essential part of human life, it should not be completely separate from home life. A complementary relationship between home and school is crucially important for the balanced development of children. Educationalists throughout history have always given importance to children's home environment and recommended a strong link between home and school. Many schools in the West have started refocusing and becoming community based. Home liaison has become one of the most important and positive steps to improving school performance and improving children's behaviour. Through Parent Teacher Associations, parents' evening and other mechanisms, schools are building better links with parents and this is paying dividends. This is fully appreciated by Muslims, as Islam has always given prime importance to a secure home environment and emphasised a holistic approach to a child's education, involving family, community and school.

Chapter Five

Home Environment

Allah has made your houses places of rest for you. (Qur'an 16:80)

Schools are centres for formal education and provide an opportunity for social interaction. However, the most important anchor in a child's life is the home. While the world around us changes and offers challenges, the home should be a sanctuary; a place where children are protected and kept away from evil. It should be a place where loving and caring adults provide a centre of joy and happiness; an abode of moral and spiritual blessing for their young ones. It is no exaggeration to say that the building block for a healthy society is a happy and stable home. Just as any organisation has a good leader at its helm, so the home has parents that provide positive examples and good strong, moral leadership.

In Islam, parents are like shepherds who are under obligation to look after the physical, emotional, moral and spiritual development of their children until they become mature. At its most basic, this means providing them with food, clothing and shelter. At its highest level, this duty of care extends to teaching and guiding them to follow in the footsteps of the noblest of human beings, the Prophet Muhammad ﷺ, and having an exemplary character. In order to best provide this care, both parents need to actively plan how to make this happen, both in the short and long term.

In addition to being a safe and confidence boosting haven, the home should serve the dual purpose of being a centre of learning and a centre of personal growth and character development.

■ As a Centre of Learning

The modern school education system is geared towards teaching our children worldly knowledge and is designed to maximise the potential of the brain, with the long-term aim of increasing economic productivity and raising the material standard of living. The moral, ethical and spiritual dimensions have been side-lined and belittled. However, no person can be whole and complete without developing the potential of the heart as well.

> **The Day when neither wealth nor sons will be of any use, except to those who come to Allah with sound and flawless hearts.** (Qur'an 26: 88-89)

It is this aspect of education that needs to be inculcated within the home environment. It is not something that can be outsourced completely to an Islamic school or madrassah once a week, although such institutions have their role to play. To this end, parents need to create an environment where children can easily gain Islamic knowledge, practice their faith and see it in action. This does not mean that every parent needs to be a scholar of Islam – just to have a willingness and intention to try their best and seek help from those that are more knowledgeable about the *deen*.

Knowledge (*'ilm*) is at the root of human superiority over other creatures. Every Muslim household should have a library at home, however small it may be, with books on Islam as well as other subjects. Parents, of course, should keep an eye on the authenticity of the sources. Partially correct or extreme views on Islam can create confusion in children and may put them off religion altogether. What is important is that children learn a love of reading, for books are the original source of knowledge and cannot be replaced by internet audios and videos.

The five pillars of Islam, when implemented correctly, teach us the value of personal sacrifice to achieve a higher non-materialistic goal as well as compassion towards other members of society. The five daily prayers give us the opportunity to reflect, be grateful and bow down in humility to The One Who created us. *Zakat* fosters a sense of brotherhood within the Ummah, while the fasts of Ramadan achieve all of these things. A practicing Muslim cannot be lazy of body or stagnant of mind or indulge in idle gossip. There is always a *salah* to be performed, *surah*s that can be memorised and *dhikr* to engage the tongue. Children have a fantastic capacity to absorb new material and the primary school years are best time to encourage memorisation of the Qur'an, simple translation, explanation and correct pronunciation of the Arabic text.

Through these continual acts of worship, we raise our standing with Allah, with our fellow human beings and, collectively, society is raised to a higher moral level. As parents, our role is to ensure that we practice this within the home to the best of our ability and teach our children, both actively and through example, how to do the same. The rest lies in Allah's hands.

As a Centre of Personal Development

Children, by nature, are restless and energetic; they always tend to be on the move. In order to harness this boundless mental and physical energy in a constructive manner, parents need to engage their children with physical and mental activities that stretch them, but not beyond their limits, to build up their skills and in turn, their confidence. This can take a variety of forms and depends on the natural inclination of the child. Outdoor activities are an essential part of childhood, providing a wholesome and healthy pastime. These can range from a walk in the park looking at nature and the changing seasons, through to martial arts and football, athletics and so on. Mental activities can take the form of activity books, puzzle games, art and craft activities.

Children should also be aware of their place and role as a valued member of the family. In an age appropriate manner, children can be asked to help with household chores and tasked with small responsibilities, such as:

- keeping their room tidy;
- helping with laying the table;
- helping to clear away the table after meals;
- putting their dirty clothes in the laundry basket;
- helping with the gardening;
- helping wash the car;
- taking responsibility for their own school uniform and school books;
- doing their homework on time;
- phoning/writing letters/making cards for grandparents or other relatives regularly.

The aim is not to tax the child unduly but to foster a sense of responsibility and belonging in the home.

Of course, however wholesome the environment at home is, the reality is that children spend about one third of their non-sleeping hours in school. They are exposed to a spectrum of other children in society from whom they learn many things and bring them home. It is important for parents to realise when their child has picked up language, a concept or a habit that is alien to Islam and moral decency. They then need to spend time explaining, with love and sensitivity, that these words or habits are not compatible with Islam. This is easiest done when parents spend quality time with their children.

QUALITY TIME WITH CHILDREN

After a long day in school many children are still energetic and they look for something to do at home in the hours before their bedtime. Unless parents can engage their children in meaningful pursuits, then these precious hours every day will be spent watching TV and playing computer games.

No doubt that this is easier said than done. All parents are busy earning their livelihoods and are additionally engaged in other social activities. It is a big job, as all parents have to earn their livelihoods and some are additionally engaged in various other works. The reality is that fathers get to spend very little quality time with their children. After a long day at work they are physically and mentally exhausted – the emotional and mental nourishment of a child does not feature high on the list of priorities. The mother alone is left to deal with feeding the family, arranging school bags for the following day, washing the dishes and so on. Little wonder then that she is tense and overworked and may take her stress out on the children. The only option for the children is to retreat into a room and watch TV or play a computer game. When both parents work, the situation is exacerbated. The result is that by the end of their primary years, children have spent hundreds of pointless hours in front of electronic gadgets and devices to no-one's benefit. The bond between parent and child becomes looser, external influences become more prominent and this can lead to major social problems in the secondary years.

Thus, spending quality time with children should not be viewed as a luxury but rather an absolute necessity. Parents need to find the balance between the needs of this world and the Hereafter. Expensive private schools alone cannot buy education and a happy future. Good degrees from good universities are not the only criterion for success in life. What is the use of life if we burn up all our energy for mere earnings and find no time for building the future?

So what does spending quality time with children actually entail? It means spending a chunk of time, sometimes one-to-one, with children that is loving and meaningful, in terms of action as well as outcome. Watching something together, telling a bedtime story, taking them out in the park, talking, chatting, laughing over family and other matters, helping with school work, all help. These activities, done little and often, create a growing bond between parent and child, build trust and love, and keep the flow of communication open.

The Prophet Muhammad ﷺ advised that those who have children should act like children with them. He used to line up the three young sons of his uncle 'Abbas and ask them to run towards him. They would run and jump on him, and he would hug and kiss them. Sometimes, he would crawl on his hands and knees while his grandchildren, Hasan and Hussain, would ride on his back.

It is all too easy for quality time to be dropped in favour of some other pressing matter. To combat this, a disciplined timetable is always a welcome addition to the family noticeboard. This can factor in parents' and children's activities, homework, *salah* times, meal times, bedtimes as well as that all important quality time. When the timetable is adhered to, it can create a sense of order and calmness, as well as a positive sense of achievement that the day has been productively spent.

Around the age of eight, children will enter into junior school and will have a greater sense of responsibility and self-discipline. It is worth inviting the input of children of this age into the family timetable and asking them how they would like to spend their quality time with their parents. Time is the most precious yet limited gift that Allah has given us. Teaching children the value of time and how to get the most out of it is one of the best skills that parents can teach to their children.

It goes without saying that parents also need to communicate with each other and discuss family issues as they arise, with or without the children present.

ISLAMIC UPBRINGING AT HOME

The manner in which children are brought up determines how they will cope in later life. In a caring, value-rich environment, where there is a sense of freedom within the broader ethos of Islam, children are less likely to be conflicted and rebellious, particularly in the challenging teenage years. On the other hand, parents who force their children and use frequent threats of punishment or 'sin' may inadvertently repel their children away altogether from religion. Of course, parents need to ensure that the basic Islamic teachings are practised in an age appropriate fashion, but the key is to lovingly advise and guide rather than impose and rebuke. For any genuine and long lasting learning to take effect, creating a positive environment is essential.

■ Islamic Rites (*Arkan*)

It is important to take things slowly because it takes time for people to embrace change. The reason why some children rebel against their parents at puberty is often because of the sudden imposition of rules without the necessary groundwork. So, for example, Islam has commanded that children must perform *salah* from the age of ten onwards, but has advised parents to begin the preparation for this from the age of seven. The Prophet Muhammad ﷺ has said:

> ***Command your children to pray at the age of seven. At the age of ten, punish them [for omitting it] and separate them in their beds.*** (Abu Dawud and al-Hakim)

Similarly, it is prudent to begin the practice of fasting or, for girls, wearing the headscarf, from before puberty, else the sudden imposition of Islamic practices at puberty is overwhelming and alien. Islamic practices should not, however, be taught as empty and meaningless rituals. They are a means of creating discipline within one's self and also within society; a means to express love and gratitude to The Creator and a means to make ourselves better human beings. These are the messages that should accompany the practice of rituals otherwise children are in danger of abandoning them once they become independent of their parents.

It is the role of parents to teach their children through words and actions and to enforce gentle, loving discipline (never physical) in order to ensure that children practice their religion. We can lead our children to the Right Path, but we cannot force them to practice. Even the Prophet Nuh عليه السلام could not save his own son, nor Prophet Lut عليه السلام his own wife.

■ Islamic Manners (*Adab*)

Islam is not just a religion of empty rituals to be performed at specific times. It is a way of life and a means to elevate the character of the individual to the highest level in every sphere of life from eating and drinking to relationships with others. When every individual in a community behaves with Islamic manners then that community as a whole is elevated. That community shines like a beacon in the dark for other communities and becomes something that others are drawn to in a positive way.

The manner in which children eat, drink, play and talk are all a reflection of their family background, home environment and innate character. Nothing is too trivial in the moulding of a fine character, as Abu Hafs 'Umar ibn Abi Salamah said:

> ***'I was a child under the care of the Prophet ﷺ. While eating, my careless hand would move around in the plate. The Prophet ﷺ said, "My son, start in the name of Allah with the right hand and take the nearest food". From then onwards I used to eat the way he taught me.'*** (al-Bukhari and Muslim)

Adab is at the heart of Muslim social life. The Prophet Muhammad ﷺ was the epitome of excellent human behaviour even before he was commissioned as a prophet. He was the kindest of his people; he served his people with humility and persistently taught them how to be good to others, without having any desire of return. Emulating him to the best of one's ability is the most rewarding goal in a Muslim's life.

These are just some of the areas in which parents should endeavour to perfect their own behaviour and teach their children:

- Greetings: How to greet other Muslims and non-Muslims; who should greet whom first and how to respond to another's greeting.
- Permission: How to seek permission to enter into someone's room or another person's house.
- Speech: How to speak in a low tone of voice; how to address others with respect and especially elders; the use of good and decent language in every day speech that is neither proud nor boastful; the use of Islamic terms within speech, such as *insha'Allah* and *masha'Allah*.

- Promises: Parents should not promise something, however trivial, to their children that they cannot fulfil otherwise it counts against them as a lie. Children should be taught to think carefully about what they promise to do and to fulfil a promise once they have made it no matter how small.
- Punctuality: Parents need to ensure that they are punctual in all their actions whether it is getting their children to school on time, performing *salah* or arriving at a function when invited by the host (not two hours later as is customary!). Children should be encouraged to play their part in assisting their parents to achieve this.
- Eating and drinking: It is good practice for a family to begin and end each meal with a *du'a*; to ensure that each and every mouthful of food consumed is not only halal but also pure (*tayyab*). Children should see and be taught the etiquette of eating with good manners and drinking while seated and of not eating on the streets.
- Mannerisms: To lower the gaze, to smile, not to walk harshly on the ground, not to whisper to one person while another is in the room, to share, not to laugh at another person's misfortune are all small but important facets of a Muslim's character, to name but a few.

Many of these things are simple every day habits that become second nature and can be carried out without effort or thought.

■ Cleanliness (*Taharah*)

Cleanliness and purity are the starting points for many acts of worship, such as *salah* and touching a *mushaf* (a printed Arabic Qur'an):

> ***The key to the Garden is prayer and the key to prayer is cleanliness.*** (at-Tirmidhi)

> **It truly is a noble Qur'an, in a well-protected Book. No one may touch it except the purified.**
> (Qur'an 56: 77-79)

Allah is Pure and loves purity and cleanliness both physical and spiritual:

> **Allah loves those who repent and loves those who purify themselves.** (Qur'an 2:222)

Thus we see from these Qur'anic *ayat* and hadith that cleanliness, both inner and outer, is an essential part of the faith, and this should be reflected in the daily activities of a Muslim.

In terms of physical cleanliness, the following habits may be helpful to implement on a regular basis:

- Obviously the Muslim home is a place where all the members of a family perform *wudu* multiple times a day. Children can also be taught *wudu* side by side with their parents at a young age to ingrain the correct procedure. It is also important to point out to children the value of using a small amount of water and the etiquette of not splashing it all over the bathroom.
- If children are given a full *ghusl* on Friday morning, it will help them to, not only learn the basics of how to perform *ghusl*, but also emphasise the importance of the day of *Jumu'ah*.
- The nails of young children should be kept clean and short and, for boys, the hair should also be kept short. For both girls and boys, the hair should be kept clean and brushed.
- Children should be dressed in clean and decent clothes from a young age. Obviously as they grow they will want more say in how they dress, but the basic rules of cleanliness and decency should still hold.

The home environment is a reflection of the people who live in it. Ideally the house should be tidy, organised and clean. This does not mean that it has to look like a show-home all the time. However, a home with piles of dirty dishes in the sink, overflowing laundry baskets and paperwork all over the place, is not a relaxing and harmonious place to live and worship. It goes without saying that the responsibility for maintaining the tidiness of the home does not just fall to the mother, but is a joint responsibility of all the family members.

■ Modesty (*Haya*)

Modesty (*haya*) is a vital ingredient in *Iman* and an inherent part of human nature. It was a natural reaction of the first human beings to cover their bodies. The following ahadith emphasise this point:

> ***Iman consists of more than sixty branches and modesty* (haya) *is a part of faith.***(al-Bukhari)
>
> ***Indecency disfigures everything and modesty* (haya) *enhances the charm of everything.*** (at-Tirmidhi)

Immodesty is rampant in the sexually permissive societies that we live in from the manner in which people dress and behave in public to the lyrics of songs and TV programming. It is therefore doubly important that we encourage modesty within our homes. Some ways in which this can be implemented are:

- Children should have separate beds by the age of ten and boys and girls should have separate bedrooms.
- All members of the family should knock on the door if they wish to enter into another person's room.
- Family members should not get dressed and undressed in front of each other and there should be a basic dress code in place for everyone. Although the rules of hijab do not apply if everyone in

the home is a *mahram*, the dress code for everyone should cover the *awrah* in a loose and opaque garment.

- Beyond the age of seven, children should not be bathed together, even those of the same sex.
- Immodest discussions should not be conducted and neither should immodest programmes and films be watched. In the same vein, a large proportion of modern lyrical music, regardless of its language, does not encourage modesty and should not have a place in the modest Muslim home.

THE ETHOS OF LISTENING

Children are not yet adults. When they talk, they often repeat things unnecessarily and sometimes talk without any clear meaning. This is how they learn to communicate with others. Parents need to have extra patience in listening to them, as active listening is a very positive skill. People have a tendency to talk more and listen less, but we should reflect on the wisdom of having two ears but only one mouth!

The art of active listening means consciously taking on board what someone is saying and understanding it. Once you really understand what someone is saying, it is easier to act on it. A parent needs to work out if their less-than-articulate child is asking for sympathy, help with a task or just needs a hug or someone to talk to.

When children are listened to, it gives them confidence that their words have some value to their parents. It also teaches them to listen when their parents talk. Active listening is the Sunnah of the Prophet ﷺ; when he listened to someone, his whole being was involved. He looked at the listener and turned his body towards them attentively. This, in turn, trains children to value others and makes them more accommodative to people around them.

When parents respond, we need to talk to our children meaningfully and in a way that they understand. The Messenger of Allah ﷺ was an active listener and a meaningful speaker:

> ***A'ishah, may Allah be pleased with her, narrated that the Prophet ﷺ spoke clearly so that all those who listened to him would understand him.*** (Abu Dawud)

A home environment in which the ethos of listening is strong, is a happier and less frustrated one as everyone feels that they have had their say.

MODERATION

Parents should treat their children as children and should not, in any way, overburden them beyond their abilities. We should not expect immediate results as working with children is a long-term investment – an investment whose return we can look forward to in later life and in the *akhirah*, insha'Allah.

Allah does not overburden His slaves (Qur'an 2:286) and we Muslims are asked to follow the middle path in all affairs of life, including how we spend money, time and energy (Qur'an 17:29, 25:67). The Prophet Muhammad ﷺ has said:

> ***A good manner of conduct, deliberation and moderation are a 24th or 25th part of Prophecy.*** (Abu Dawud and at-Tirmidhi)

Whenever the Messenger of Allah ﷺ was given the choice of one of two matters, he would choose the easier of the two, as long as it was not wrongful to do so, but if it was wrongful to do so he would not approach it. (al-Bukhari)

Expecting children to excel at school in every subject or to practice all aspects of the *deen* perfectly is counterproductive. Children are a work in progress. It is our job to bring the best out of them, not to crush them under the pressure of our high expectations. Not only does this destroy the spirit of the child, it also leads to strained parent-child relationships. Moderation in all matters creates ease.

DEALING WITH DIFFICULT BEHAVIOUR

Even children raised in a wholesome Islamic environment struggle to cope with the pull of society. Although the years of the toddler temper tantrums may have passed, behavioural problems will arise in the home. Whatever the problem, parents should not be judgemental about their children. Problems can be one-off, due to psychological reasons or external factors. They may be quite different from those which are deliberate or which have patterns. Parents should categorise any problem on the basis of its:

- severity
- frequency
- duration
- persistence

Dealing with problems depends on the context, the parent-child relationship and the intellectual maturity of the child. Should a problem arise, it is important for the parents not to lose their temper, shout or blame. Children should be helped to realise their own mistakes. In any case they should not be humiliated or denigrated in their sense of self-worth. Confident and proud Muslim children will understand the consequences of their mistakes and try to repair and rebuild themselves.

Managing challenging behaviour from one's children needs extra patience, as parents normally have high expectations of their own children and if anything goes wrong in their behaviour they become upset. We often forget that 'to err is human'; we have a tendency to look for perfection in our loved ones, when we ourselves fail to maintain high standards. This is when the ethos of listening and moderation come in useful. In addition, the following 6 Cs are important to remember when any unfortunate behavioural problems of our children occur:

- Calmness – do not resort to shouting.
- Confidence – you, as the parent, have the ability to deal effectively with this problem.
- Consistency – the child should receive a clear and consistent message about what constitutes acceptable behaviour.
- Clarity – do not allow your emotions to cloud your judgement.
- Control – do not succumb to anger and violence.
- Communication – keep the lines of communication open with your spouse as to how to deal with the issue and also with the child according to the ethos of active learning.

CULTURE AND THE MOTHER TONGUE

I want to touch briefly on the role of culture and the mother tongue within the Islamic home environment. Of course, the rules and regulations set forth within Islam offer the guiding principles for the Muslim home. Anything prohibited in Islam is haram no matter how much a part of the culture 'back home' it may be. However, the beauty of the Muslim Ummah is in its diversity of dress, language, food and customs and the thread that binds us is our common practice of Islam.

It is not contradictory to create an Islamic home environment in which the cultural and linguistic roots of the parents are also given importance. In fact this is an essential part of a pluralistic society and forms part of the colourful mosaic that makes up a human being.

Knowledge of the Arabic language is essential in the understanding of the Qur'an and every Muslim child should have a working knowledge of the Qur'anic Arabic language. However, the mother tongue also has a role to play in anchoring children, in helping them to communicate with their elders and other relatives. Most Muslim community languages are respectful, historically rich and carry the Islamic message by default.

HALAL AND HARAM

Ultimately, it is not the size of the house nor the possessions in it that define a home. A home and its inhabitants will be showered with Allah's blessing only when it is founded upon all that is halal and pure.

Abu Hurayrah ﷺ said: the Messenger of Allah ﷺ said: "O people, Allah is Good and only accepts that which is good. Allah commanded the pious to follow the same commandments as He gave to the Messengers. He says (interpretation of the meaning):

> **'O (you) Messengers! Eat of the Tayyibat [all kinds of Halal (lawful) foods which Allah has made lawful (meat of slaughtered eatable animals, milk products, fats, vegetables, fruits)] and do righteous deeds. Verily, I am Well-Acquainted with what you do'** (Qur'an 23:51)

> **'O you who believe! Eat of the lawful things that We have provided you with'** (Qur'an 2:172)

> ***Then he mentioned a man who has travelled on a long journey and is dishevelled and covered with dust; he stretches forth his hands to the heaven, (saying) "O Lord, O Lord", but his food is haram, his drink is***

haram, all his nourishment is haram, so how can his du'a be accepted?" (Muslim)

In order to have a blessed home, it is vital to earn a halal income through one's own hard work in a halal environment. In fact, it is an act of worship for a man to earn and spend on his own family. It is then equally important to spend and save that income in a halal manner. This means that savings should not attract interest. Money should be spent on halal and pure ingredients because 'the flesh nourished from haram food will not have its place in the Garden, and the Fire is its abode' (Ahmad, ad-Darimi, al-Bayhaqi). There should be moderation in the amount of money that is spent on entertainment or fashion and other things that are of little spiritual benefit. A portion of a family's wealth should be set aside for *zakat* and *sadaqah* in order to purify it. Insha'Allah these actions will be a source of abundance and protection for the home and family.

SUMMARY

Like dry sponges children's brains absorbs whatever they see or hear. This remains imprinted for a long time. Parents and other adults should be able to display good behaviour, such as respect and tolerance, in order to give them a good education and the joy of childhood. They should try to create a learning and joyful environment at home so that whatever they see or hear is positive. Prophet Muhammad's ﷺ dealings with his two grandchildren, Hasan and Hussein, were full of love and mercy. On one occasion he lengthened his prostration (*sajdah*) while performing in prayer, his companions asked him about this. The Prophet ﷺ answered, 'My grandson rode on my back and I gave him time to play'.

Chapter Six

Building Muslim Character

"My son, do not associate any partner with Allah. Associating others with Him is a terrible wrong... My son, establish prayer and enjoin right and forbid wrong and be steadfast in the face of what befalls you. That is certainly the most resolute course to follow. Do not turn your cheek from people out of haughtiness and do not walk with arrogance in the land. Allah does not love anyone who is boastful. Be moderate in your tread and lower your voice. The most hateful of voices is the donkey's bray." (Qur'an 31:13-19)

EDUCATION: THE WESTERN PERSPECTIVE

Modern Western education has proved effective in providing the younger generation with key skills, such as communication and information-processing skills, reasoning and problem-solving skills, social and life skills, and creative thinking and evaluation skills. However, all of the above are geared to survival and success in a secular society, where the emphasis is on making an economic contribution to society while amassing as much personal material gain as possible.

The main focus of Western education is to produce 'good citizens', primarily to sustain and improve economic productivity and effectively play their citizenship roles. The state and society invests energy to make sure this is achieved. The debate and discussion on education is always centred round buzz words like 'standards', 'excellence' and 'performance'. As a result, teachers are under immense pressure to produce better measurable educational standards in schools, colleges and universities that can be reflected in league tables. This pressure together with ever increasing amounts of paperwork and a lack of respect that teachers often face, means that Western education is not addressing the holistic needs of a child as much as it could.

ISLAMIC EDUCATION: A HOLISTIC APPROACH

The purpose of education is to transmit a philosophy of life to new generations and prepare them for the future. It creates a link between generations whereby the elder generation passes down their knowledge and experience while learning from the innovative and creative younger generation. An education system reflects the prevailing attitudes, the cultural and historical legacy of a nation. It takes into account the norms and values of society at that time.

It is not enough to simply transmit the latest scientific or economic or medical concepts down the generations. Recently, citizenship lessons have introduced concepts into the classroom such as loyalty, liberty, justice, diversity and fairness. However, the tie that binds all these concepts and gives them meaning is knowledge of the human purpose on earth. If any education system ignores why we have been created and what we have been put on the earth to do, then all this secular knowledge brings no ultimate benefit.

It is vitally important for children to receive an education in the arts and sciences of the world but this must rest on a strong foundation of moral, spiritual and ethical knowledge and practice, and that foundation has to be built at the very beginning of their lives. In practical terms this means that young people should pursue careers in any and every field that is not haram but always carrying in the forefront of their mind the firm belief in the All-Powerful and Ever-Vigilant Creator from Whom they came and to Whom they will return. This belief acts as a rope that young people can hold onto throughout their lives; a guide that will give them stability, dignity and conviction and will never see them wander far from The Straight Path. They will always be mindful of their responsibility to others and their accountability to Allah. So while their secular counterparts are slaves to the ever-changing whims and desires of society and wealth and fashions, the holistically educated young person will be insha'Allah successful and fulfilled, not only in this *dunya*, but where it really matters – the *akhirah*.

In the history of Islam, the most successful periods of education have always seen investment in the arts, physical and biological sciences and medicine as well as the theological. Muslim society was the richer for having struck a balance between the two. European academics travelled to the centres of Islamic learning to gain the worldly knowledge that was missing in the Dark Ages of Mediaeval Europe while society lived in prosperity and harmony because it understood and adhered to Islamic principles. Decline set into those enriched societies only when the balance of the two was disturbed.

Islamic education should therefore not be thought of as simply acquiring an in-depth knowledge of the Qur'an, hadith, *fiqh* and *Shariah*. Rather it is the acquisition of all knowledge available to human beings together with its sincere practice for the multiple aims of serving Allah, serving other people, making a contribution to society and a level of personal gain, both in terms of money and self-fulfilment.

There is clear unanimity among Muslim scholars that education should aim at familiarising individuals with:

- the rights that are due to Allah (*huqooq Allah*);
- the rights that are due to other human beings (*huqooq al-'Ibad*). This ranges from our behaviour, attitude and responsibilities towards our immediate family, extended family, wider community, guests, travellers, the poor and needy, orphans, widows, fellow Muslims, non-Muslims;
- the rights that are due to other creatures/animals and to the environment;
- our relationship to the universe and exploration of natural and physical laws in order to utilise them;
- deep appreciation of the Maker's creative wisdom and a study of His creation.

So how can we as parents achieve this on a practical level with our children in the present day?

PARENTAL ROLE IN BUILDING MUSLIM CHARACTER

It is clear that we cannot rely on schools alone to provide our children with all the elements that comprise education and so we need to supplement our children's education during the times that they are not at school.

Building Muslim character needs constant and conscious training and practice on the parts of both parents and children. Effective training requires competent trainers with excellent personal qualities that inspire trust and confidence. This is why it is said that it takes a whole village to raise a child. A child that has access to a variety of inspiring role models will always have somewhere to turn and take direction from.

So as a first step, we parents need to work out what resources we have: how much time can we spend with our children and do we have the required level of knowledge to impart to them? What external resources can we make use of, such as family, other community members, the local mosque, weekend/evening Islamic schools?

Ideally, it is the parents that are the first teachers, educators and role models for their sons and daughters. Parents, and especially the mother, have a unique love and affection for their children that no one else can possess. Raising a successful generation of Muslims therefore depends on that love and affection being available to the child right from when they are in the womb. It is love and kindness that teaches the most effective lessons not fear and harshness.

The following are a number of tried and tested training methods that can be adopted at home to build Muslim character:

➔ **Advice, Persuasion and Reminder** – All the Prophets and wise people on earth adopted this basic technique to train their people. The Qur'an mentions Luqman's excellent advice to his son. For maximum benefit, advice should be timely, relevant and consistent. The Prophet Muhammad ﷺ advised people, individually and collectively, in a way that had lasting impact on them, but never with harshness. Parents are in an excellent position to do this day in and day out.

➔ **Parables and Storytelling** – The Qur'an tells the stories of past nations in an eloquent manner with a view to remind people so that they reflect and learn. The parables, such as a 'pure tree' for a 'good word' and a 'bad tree' for an 'evil word' mentioned in the Qur'an, is a beautiful example (Qur'an 14:24-26). Prophets Jesus ('Isa) ﷺ and Muhammad ﷺ used good parables to clarify things to their companions. On one occasion the Prophet Muhammad ﷺ used a comparison between a human being's capacity to use knowledge and the soil's response to rain. Parables, metaphors and stories have a greater impact on the memory and help them understand the meaning of life. Muslim parents should be the source of good parables and stories. Bedtime stories for younger children have proved effective in all cultures.

➔ **Role Modelling** – The Prophet Muhammad ﷺ has been sent as the model for humanity (Qur'an 33:21). He took part in mundane work with his companions, for example, building the mosque at Madinah, digging the ditch in preparation to defend his city against the enemy and on many other occasions, where he was no different from his companions. He was the perfect father, husband and companion. Role models have tremendous influence on the attitudes and actions of a child. Parents can be exemplary role models for their children.

➔ **Rewards and Sanctions** – Allah has created the Garden to reward people who have true faith (*iman*) in Him and do right actions, and the Fire to punish people who reject faith and do wrong actions. The Prophet Muhammad ﷺ used to give recognition to the good works of his companions and sometimes disciplined them for wrong or unacceptable behaviour and action. The story of the three companions who were penalised for failing to participate in the expedition to Tabuk is an example. Rewards and sanctions are effective tools to teach young children about the reality of life. Sanctions should always be carried out firmly and with love, explaining to the child that it is only their behaviour that is unacceptable, but the child is loved unconditionally.

Other activities that can be incorporated in the daily routine include:

- Follow Allah's guidance and the Sunnah of the Prophet ﷺ in our daily activities so that children emulate this too. This includes the main Islamic rites, remembrance of Allah, supplication and the *Masnoon Du'a* (supplications from the Sunnah) for any event or incident, as taught by the Prophet ﷺ.
- Establish *salah* on time. It is helpful to set up an *adhan* clock to hear the call to prayer five times a day as reminder. If the mosque is near, fathers should take their children to the congregational prayers.
- Refer to Qur'an and Sunnah when talking about issues of relevance. They are the reference points for Muslims. Copies of the Qur'an and collections of ahadith should be in every house and used as a reference regularly.
- Make a practice of regular recitation of the Qur'an at home so that children develop this habit. Make use of time spent in the car to listen to the Qur'an on CD.
- Encourage children to reflect on the miracles of creation. Our whole existence and surroundings testify to the miracles of Allah. Take walks to appreciate the changing seasons of nature or grow seeds in the garden or window boxes.
- Socialise with practising Muslim families so that children can pick their closest friends from them. This is important for their confidence in early childhood. Their ability to interact with the wider society later on will thus be enhanced. This will also create a network support for the parents to have like-minded families.

- Maintain a cordial relationship with neighbours. This will create socialisation skills in the child and a tendency to help others in their need. This service (*khidmah*) aspect of Islam is at the heart of the Prophetic Sunnah and a major ingredient of a happy community.
- Arrange regular family sessions. They help family bonding and increase knowledge of and conviction in Islam. Parents can encourage their children in family affairs through discussion in family issues and mutual consultation as was the way of the Prophet ﷺ.
- Arrange healthy competition among the siblings on knowledge, such as quiz evening or memorisation competitions. Competition in knowledge and *taqwa* is encouraged in Islam and it pushes young people forward.
- Educate children about the Muslim world and its history as well as contemporary world in order to create an interest in them for engaging in the intellectual, socio-political and financial betterment of the ummah. Keep abreast of current affairs programmes through newspapers and TV from a variety of sources so children (and us) are aware of what is going on in the world.
- Provide positive recreation so that children are kept away from indecent and sensual pleasures. Arts and crafts projects, gardening, cooking, growing their own, reading, visiting farms, parks are all useful and fun activities.

SUPPLEMENTARY ISLAMIC SCHOOLING

Of course, parents cannot always provide all aspects of a spiritual education at home and this is where they may consider evening or weekend Islamic schools or madrassahs where children can be taught

Qur'an and Islamic Studies. It can sometimes be difficult to put aside a regular time to teach children at home or parents may not feel confident in teaching these subjects to their children, so these Islamic schools have a vital role to play in the religious education of our children. In addition, they provide the opportunity for Muslim families within the same locality to meet and socialise and strengthen community ties and access to teachers who can impart knowledge to our children and be good role models to them.

In making the decision to send their child to an evening or weekend school, parents need to consider the following points:

- Children attend school for seven hours a day, five days a week and they come home tired and often with homework. It is important that they have a chance to recharge physically and mentally in the evenings and at weekends. Parents should pay attention to the timings and length of the Islamic class and ensure that the child is not overtired because of their schedule.
- Parents should visit the building where classes take place and be aware of how much space and resources are available to the children for learning. An overcrowded classroom with just a whiteboard and pen is not necessarily the most conducive environment for learning.
- Parents should also ideally be able to see a class in progress or at least speak to the teachers and management staff. Many supplementary Islamic schools, albeit with the best of intentions, are largely run by non-professional teachers, who may not have enough knowledge of modern classroom management. They may not have the experience on how to deal with behavioural issues or have the time for developing motivating and inspiring lesson plans.

Parents often just send their children to the local madrassah class once a week when they reach a certain age so that they can be free of the responsibility of providing their children with Islamic education at home. First of all, religion is not something that can be learnt in a 2-3 hour session per week. An evening or weekend madrassah is just one of the resources that can be used to help parents in a larger framework. Secondly, children who are forced to attend under-resourced, badly managed and poorly taught lessons will be left with a negative image of religion. In this case, parents can:

- Make the effort to teach their children at home in an inspiring and motivated way using the many resources that are now available, such as reward stickers, posters, colourful books and Islamic toys.
- Consider one-to-one or small group tutoring in which one teacher imparts knowledge either in their own home or the child's. Parents can speak with potential teachers to assess their suitability and have more control over the manner in which their child is taught.
- If the local madrassah is struggling with resources and motivated teachers, then parents can offer their help to improve these or establish new ones in areas where they do not exist. The positive and proactive parent realises that, in the long-term, the Muslim community does need these schools that provide a focus for the Muslim community. Through our communal efforts, insha'Allah, there can be a thriving weekend school in every locality that our children look forward to attending.

CREATING A MUSLIM YOUTH CULTURE

Our role as Muslim parents is to ensure that our children are confident and assured within themselves and in their identity. When they are at peace within themselves, then they will be able to make a positive contribution to the well-being of the society they live in on many levels. They can look forward to making an economic contribution through their jobs in whatever field they choose; they will be sensitive enough to want to help the less fortunate members of society with their time, effort and skills; they will insha'Allah grow up to be balanced adults, spouses and parents who will elevate the future generations.

This can only be achieved if we work tirelessly NOW to instil a Muslim youth culture in our children of which they and we can be proud: a culture where every child feels loved within their immediate family, feels that they have a valued role within the wider community and a support network of friends and adults to whom they can turn when they feel unsure. We need to make sure that our children are proud to be Muslim, not apologetic or ashamed, and we need to inspire them to love Islam and all that it is. This can be done on many levels but requires constant effort on the part of the parents.

In creating a Muslim culture, I am not suggesting for one moment that Muslims isolate themselves or restrict their social circle and friendships to one ethnic or religious group. This is against the spirit of Islam in which it is important to interact with the wider society and to be of service to others. However, the world around us can be an overwhelming and confusing place for a young person. There is much that looks alluring but is in fact immoral. We want our young people to be secure and anchored within their own identity and principles before they are exposed to wider society so that they do not blow aimlessly like leaves in the wind succumbing to external pressures, but rather they shine like candles.

■ The Role of the Mosque and Youth Organisations

Taking children to mosques and Islamic centres from a young age opens the door to a wider world with people of diverse backgrounds. Mosques have been the central institution for education and creating a community spirit in Islamic history. Unfortunately many mosques are very quiet today and even kept locked outside prayer times. Regeneration of the Ummah will remain a dream if mosques are used as places of ritual prayer alone. Mosques must be brought back to play their full role, as was exemplified by the Messenger's Mosque in Madinah. In addition to congregational prayers and Qur'an classes, they should organise a host of activities, for example, sports, discussion groups and supplementary classes.

The best way to harness the potential of Muslim children is to involve them in Islamic circles from an early age, where they can be engaged in a host of positive activities. The Prophet Muhammad ﷺ revived and initiated social welfare work through an association called Hilf al-Fudul, in his youth. Parents should encourage their children to join groups related to mosques or reputable Muslim organisations. Junior groups, like the Junior Muslim Circle (JMC) based in East London, can engage very young children in challenging activities and create motivation in them to grow with a positive ethos of life when they are still young and innocent. Ideally, Muslim youth organisations should aspire to provide the following services:

- organising social events;
- organising classes on Qur'an, Islamic knowledge, the Arabic language and spiritual development;
- organising sports, leisure and entertainment activities;
- organising campaigns against anti-social activities;
- advising and helping young people in their homework and career guidance;
- organising training and leadership programmes.

They also create opportunities to make friendship with others around them, which is very important for their social life. Children easily make and break friends and through this they learn about themselves and the world around them. Parents can and should help their young ones to choose suitable friends since peer pressure can be a very powerful factor in how children behave.

■ Celebrations

Every community has its festivals and the Muslims have our two Eids: one, after the month-long fasting of Ramadan and the other to commemorate the sacrifice of the Prophet Ibrahim عليه السلام after the Day of Arafat. Both these social occasions are meant to make an imprint on Muslim children of remembrance and worship of Allah with the wider Muslim community, and also having fun. Islamic recreation has a unique moral and spiritual dimension; Muslim parents should provide their children with the opportunity to enjoy it fully and to create a feeling of togetherness among Muslims all over the world.

Parents can:

- Explain through role playing and story-telling the reason for celebrating the two Eids;
- Decorate the house;
- Make cards and give gifts to family, friends and the less fortunate in society;
- Take the day off school and work;
- Make or buy new clothes;
- Plan the day to include going to the mosque, visiting family and friends and having a fun activity scheduled for the children.

■ Holidays

School holidays are the time where parents can really concentrate on activities for the children as they are not tired from the pressures of school and schoolwork. Holidays need to be planned with innovative thinking if parents want to keep their children happy and busy. Of course, if the family budget allows, parents can take their children on holidays abroad to countries such as Turkey, Spain, Morocco and Iran, to name but a few. There is a wealth of Islamic history, culture and architecture in these countries that will bring the glorious past to life. It is wonderful to be able to take children on *'Umrah* to follow in the footsteps of the prophets or perhaps to their country of origin where there are relatives that they can connect with.

Closer to home, there are places of outstanding natural beauty where the wonders of Allah's creation are apparent away from the hustle and bustle of city life. There are also a number of Islamic camps and retreats that provide a holiday with a spiritual dimension and activities for the whole family.

Children can have a great deal of fun and playful learning without leaving home if parents can make the effort to provide children with positive and beneficial activities to do each day. It would be a shame if the precious weeks of relaxation of a child's holidays were spent in front of the TV and computer with no opportunity for personal growth, human interaction and real fun.

Chapter Seven

Conclusion

In this book, I have attempted to discuss parenting as an obligatory task which is linked with the purpose of human life on earth. To Muslims, parenting is important not only for our *dunya*, but also the *akhirah*. The Qur'an tells us that children are a 'test' and 'trust' for Muslim parents. It is an immense responsibility entrusted by Allah to us. The purpose of parenting is to develop effective emissaries of Allah on earth through love, care and proper education and training. Allah wants us to strive as best as we can to keep this earth as His well-managed 'garden'. Effective parenting means passing on positive and universal values, ethos and a sense of responsibility to children. The family as an institution in which fathers and mothers create a happy, joyful and learning atmosphere is central. A loving and caring family environment anchors young people to their parents and family members, through which they learn to love their community and other human beings. This should be embedded in Muslim nature and is the essence of Islamic social life. On the other hand, those who grow with neglectful or rigid parents or are raised in unstable environments suffer and are less likely to contribute to society, even becoming a burden on it. Deprivation is not only economic and social, it can be moral and spiritual as well. Socio-economic deprivation creates chaos in the society, and moral and spiritual deprivation brings confusion and loss of humanity. No individual or society can prosper under these conditions.

I have also attempted to bring home the fact that parenting is fundamentally an assertive, interactive and proactive endeavour that needs strategies, forward planning, continuous alertness, enterprise and undiluted commitment – day in and day out. Parenting starts from the moment a baby is conceived in the mother's womb and is a life-long process. It involves physical sustenance, emotional support, social upbringing and spiritual nourishment of the young from their earliest years. The commitment involved in parenting at different stages of a child's life brings new challenges, adventures, joy and happiness. The reward is enormous - a sense of achievement in this world and the pleasure of Allah in the Hereafter.

SUMMARY OF GUIDELINES

Parents have authority over their children. It needs to be used conscientiously and effectively. Here are a few helpful tips on how to use this authority for children's wholesome growth.

Parents should:

- Make an early start in educating their children and giving them the understanding of Islam and the world, before it is too late. Children should be told about the history of Islam and pioneering Muslims, so that they can take them as role models. Stories from the Qur'an and ahadith have tremendous influence on young minds and once the foundation is laid, they are less likely to slip away from Islamic moorings.

- Encourage children to practise Islam with spirit. According to the Prophet Muhammad's ﷺ instructions, parents should begin teaching the children prayer at the age of seven. By ten, they should be disciplined for failure to do so.
- Understand the psychology of young children in order to deal with them effectively. Simple observation and common sense are required.
- Allow them innocent or meaningful fun. Children like to enjoy themselves. Parents should direct them to sensible enjoyment, otherwise they will be bored and might find their own. The Prophet Muhammad ﷺ asked Muslims to treat children as they are.
- Establish a good pattern of parenting so that children know their boundaries. Parenting that lacks discipline is bound to create confusion in the children.
- Watch their moods and be consistent in dealing with their words and actions so that the children feel comfortable. Constantly changing rules or moving goalposts confuses children. Intelligent children observe their parents to see how consistent they are. Consistency does not mean rigidity. If rules are changed, this must be explained to the children.
- Refrain from giving orders to children. If we want children to do something we should use convincing methods. Explanations are sometimes necessary. Parents should try to use persuasion so that the children do things on their own accord.
- Be in control of children. New to life as they are, children need guidance from experienced people. As such, appropriate control is essential for their benefit. However, attempting too much to control may be counterproductive.

- Keep promises, even if difficult or costly. Breaking promises can be disheartening to children as they may take it as lying, which is forbidden in Islam, and will also break a child's trust in a parent.
- Use moderation in behaviour towards children. Too much liberty may spoil them and on the other hand, too much rigidity may make them rebellious. Islam is about moderation in life and children should not grow up in extremes.
- Be forthright in action. Efforts to hide things from children can have disastrous effects. They can gradually lose confidence in their parents.
- Speak simply and clearly so that the children learn to do the same. Straightforward and simple language encourages children to become positive.
- Listen to children when they talk. Interrupting them encourages them to do the same when their parents or elders talk.
- Arrange family sessions on important issues regularly. Through engagement in wholesome discussion, parents can create interest in children and foster their sense as a valuable family member.
- Accept mistakes. Children should know that no human being, including their parents, is perfect. When parents accept their mistakes, this gives them confidence on parental judgement and they will not view them as unfair.
- Be sensitive to children's feelings. Children have good and bad times and as such, they need space. Adults have good and bad days and so too should children be allowed to have natural ups and downs.
- Involve them in wholesome activities, such as easy household work, so that they feel the sense of belonging at home. It also increases their self-esteem and confidence.

- Treat children equally (Ahmad, Abu Dawud and an-Nasa'i). It is cruel to show love and attention to one child and indifference to another. This creates jealousy and hatred among siblings.
- Play a positive role in helping children to select their friends and peer group on the basis of mannerisms, good Islamic and human character.
- Help them find real-life role models from among family members and the wider community of exemplary character.
- Be pro-active in dealing with sensitive issues. When children grow, especially towards the end of their primary school life, fathers and mothers should divide their attention between their sons and daughters respectively in order to educate them in sensitive issues such as sex.
- Discuss together the strategy of educating and disciplining the children and speak with one voice. Children must not be given the impression that one parent is softer or stricter than the other. They may play parents against each other. Should any disagreement arise on any issue, the parents need to discuss them privately, not in front of the children.
- Reward children for being good. This gives them inner happiness and encourages them to keep on doing good things. It also gives them confidence that they are valued. However, parents must be careful that they do not bribe their children and spoil them.
- Discipline but do not punish them if children do something unworthy. Justice must be maintained while disciplining children, and both parents should be involved in the process. Parents who have a well-balanced policy of discipline know when and how they should implement it. Unless something is serious, the natural sequence of disciplining is – a) showing disapproval, b) giving a caution and finally c) withholding privileges.

- Teach children to apologise and accept their apologies. This develops their conscience. Once they apologise, parents should readily accept their apologies without going into details. Children should also be taught to ask forgiveness from Allah. Conversely, if parents make a mistake they should not be too proud to apologise to their children.
- Maintain good relationships with their teachers in order to learn how the children are doing academically and socially. Children, whose parents do talk to teachers, are better looked after in school.

And remember - enjoy the company of your child(ren)! You will never be loved and looked up to as much by anyone else. It really is a privilege to be a parent, so please enjoy these precious years.

Our children are the greatest assets that Allah has entrusted us with. We owe it to Allah and to our children, therefore, to invest our time and efforts into being the best parents we can be. **Cherishing Childhood** is a parent-to-parent handbook that outlines how to tackle the challenges (and reap the rewards) of parenting children from birth to pre-adolescence within an Islamic ethos in a pluralist society.

It covers:

» The concept of Positive Parenting;
» How to welcome a child into the world;
» The unique nature of a toddler and how to manage the most common issues in the pre-school years;
» Matters to consider when choosing a primary school;
» How to support your child through primary school;
» Creating the most nurturing home environment for children to flourish in;
» Guidelines for discipline and dealing with difficult behaviour;
» Tips on how to build a Muslim character.

Dr. Muhammad Abdul Bari is an educationalist and community activist holding a PhD and PGCE from King's College London and a Management degree from the Open University. He has worked as an Air Force Officer, researcher in physics, science teacher and a behaviour support teacher. He was Secretary General of the Muslim Council of Britain (2006-10), Chairman of the East London Mosque Trust (2002-13) and a board member of the London Olympics and Paralympics Organising Committee (2006-13). He writes on community and social issues and has authored several books on Muslim family, parenting and identity. He is the founder of **AmanaParenting** and **Head2Heart** (a socio-political forum). He is married with four children.

Ta–Ha Publishers Ltd
Unit 4, The Windsor Centre
Windsor Grove
London, SE27 9NT
United Kingdom

ISBN 978-1-84200-154-7